CHASTITY AND THE AFFECTIVE LIFE

Chastity and the Affective Life

Albert Plé

Translated by
Marie-Claude Thompson

HERDER AND HERDER

1966
HERDER AND HERDER NEW YORK
232 Madison Avenue, New York 10016

Original edition: *Vie Affective et Chasteté*,
Paris, Editions du Cerf, 1964.

Imprimi Potest:	J. Kopf, O.P.
	Provincial
Nihil Obstat:	Thomas J. Beary
	Censor Librorum
Imprimatur:	✠ Robert F. Joyce
	Bishop of Burlington
	April 21, 1966

The *Nihil obstat* and *Imprimatur* are official declarations that a book or
pamphlet is considered to be free of doctrinal or moral error. No implica-
tion is contained therein that those who have granted the *Nihil obstat* and
Imprimatur agree with the contents, opinions, or statements expressed.

Contents

CONTENTS

CHASTITY AND THE AFFECTIVE LIFE

Introduction
"You Shall Love"

DURING the fifteenth and sixteenth centuries it became customary in the Church to teach morality and Christian life in its entirety using the commandments of God as the basic scheme, that is, the commandments of the Old Testament, though modified somewhat by the teachings of the New Testament.

The focal status thus afforded to the Decalogue can easily be understood from pedagogical considerations. By basing the teaching of morality on the commandments, one could be assured of solid foundations for a morality which was in large measure natural, but Christianized by the additional teaching of the commandments of the Church. This method of pedagogy met the most urgent and most fundamental social needs of the Christian community; for a morality common to an entire civilization must both be grounded on natural principles and not lack a body of prescriptions and practices; these manifest and strengthen the "closed morality" so forcefully described by Bergson.

Such a morality controls people, creates order, and ensures a solid foundation for proper behavior. In league with a strong piety, it can build and sustain the life of very vigorous Christian communities. Proof of this is to be found not only in the Christendom of the Middle Ages, but even in our own day, for example in such countries as Ireland and Canada, or in the Catholicism of the United States.

Historically, this method of teaching Catholic morality appears as a new phenomenon: it is a product of the decadent Middle Ages.[1]

[1] The first systematization of this conception of morality seems to be the work of William of Ockham (in the first half of the fourteenth century); see L. Vereecke, "L'obligation morale selon Guillaume d'Ockham," in *Supplément de la Vie Spirituelle*, no. 45 (1958).

As a matter of fact, not to speak of the Fathers and of the first theologians, the first great systematization of Christian morality, that of St. Thomas Aquinas, is organized not around the Decalogue, but around the desire for beatitude and grace, human acts, and virtues and vices. Unfortunately, this dynamic structuring of morality has not been widespread in the Church, which has preferred to it a systematization built upon the commandments. The Decalogue, despite the definite pedagogical advantages it provides, has its dangers, its lacunae, its distortions, which we must have the courage to face.

When, in the fifteenth and sixteenth centuries, the commandments of God were taken as the outline of the teaching of morality, it was not possible to avoid the danger of putting excessive emphasis on the law (and on a juridical mentality). Generation after generation, the enthusiasm for Roman juridicism (take, for example, the "legists" of Philippe le Bel, or the higher officials of the royalty, or even the "Roman" spirit of the republicans of 1789), and then the parallel vogue of Stoicism (which so strongly influenced most of the great minds of the Renaissance and of the Revolution) increased this emphasis. This reduction of morality to law and duty grew further during the nineteenth century, as the effect of a moral ideal required by the Kantian imperative.

The result was that the criterion of morality was increasingly limited to an external conformity to the moral law. At the same time, the moral law hardened and became more and more precise in its smallest details to the point of constituting a sort of code of the same nature as that of civil laws, without any vital communication, either with moral conscience and man's psychological dynamism or with the spirit of the Gospel. From this conjuncture arose casuistry and the nominalistic, legalistic, and rationalistic teaching of Christian morality.

Thus step by step the Church has drifted towards a teaching of the morality of Christ impoverished of what is most Christian and most evangelistical in it. The moral teaching in our catechisms comes close to scandal.[2]

No matter what the reasons for this infidelity to the Gospel are,

---

[2] See, for example, H. Woroniecki, "La place des préceptes de charité dans l'enseignement du catéchisme," in *Angelicum* XV (1948, 1) pp. 18–26.

the situation is now such that, from children in catechism classes to seminarians, from parishioners to monks and nuns, we are all "educated" by a legalistic morality whose insufficiencies and particular inopportuneness can no longer be tolerated.

A "legalistic" morality leads directly to Pharisaism, that is to say, to the reduction of our relations with God to the observance—zealous, but material—of a moral and religious code. He who follows this code avoids with difficulty the temptation of taking comfort and vanity from a perfection which he finds in himself; he no longer recognizes himself as a sinner,[3] he no longer expects his justification from God alone, the justification which comes from the faith in Jesus Christ (Rom. 3, 22), who has become "our wisdom, our righteousness and sanctification and redemption; therefore, as it is written, 'Let him who boasts, boast of the Lord' " (1 Cor. 1, 30–31).

In spite of his apparent zeal for God, the Pharisee expects from his works only a perfection which is but human and of which we must even say that it is practically atheistic. On the contrary, an authentic moral life receives its inner dynamism from union with God; Catholic morality is fundamentally a divine life, a *"mystique,"* a divine morality, divine in its source as in its end: it is *first* a gift of God (Rom. 5, 17) and a gratuitous gift of God (Rom. 6, 13), that is to say a grace (Rom. 6, 14), an act of mercy (Rom. 9, 15–18); it is a new birth (Jn. 3, 3), a life "according to the Spirit" (Rom. 8 *passim,* esp. 18–27), a faith (Rom. 3, 22), a hope (Rom. 8, 18–27), a love (Rom. 8, 35–39).

Only afterwards is Christian morality a morality of practices and observances: they are the "fruit for God" (Rom. 7, 4) of this morality, not its sap. If this "afterwards" becomes a "beforehand," Christian morality drifts towards the moral legalism and rationalism of the preceding centuries. Whatever of theocentric quality (dissolved in a sentimental piety) remains in it can maintain, indeed, a few pulsations of Christian life; but he for whom Christianity is reduced negatively to the (conceptual) refusal of theft, murder and adultery,

[3] E. Roche, "Notre condition de pécheurs," in *Nouvelle revue théologique* (juillet-août, 1950) pp. 690–703.

and positively to Mass on Sunday and abstinence from meat on Friday, is moribund in his Christian life.

It is true that human mediocrity and misery are sufficient to explain this Christian asthenia, but do we not have to recognize that they are encouraged in a certain way by a teaching of morality based on the commandments, or even practically limited to them?

In fact, insofar as this legalization of morality constitutes a sort of regression of the Gospel to the Old Testament, it is subject to the affirmations, audacious but so terrifying in their truth, which St. Paul addresses to the law:

I had not known sin save through the Law. For I had not known lust unless the Law had said, "You shall not lust." But sin, having seized a base of operations in the commandment, produced in me by its means all manner of lust, for without law sin lies dormant. Once too I was without law, but when the commandment came, sin was stirred to life, and I died. Thus the commandment that was to lead to life, was discovered in my case to lead to death. Sin, having seized a base of operations in the commandment, deceived me, and thereby killed me" [Rom. 7, 7–11].

It is an experiential truth that the seduction of sin takes advantage of the commandment. Some psychoanalysts think that they are the first to discover this truth, which they blame on an education which they believe Christian when it is but the fruit of a pseudo-morality[4] based on an absolute imperative foreign to the psychological dynamism of the subject.

If moral law is but this foreign body, this "super-ego" introjected into the child's ego by parental interdictions, by the identification with the father and the mother or their substitutes, then to become an adult and "conquer one's personality" is to reject this exogenous and destructive substance. What is forbidden thus becomes what is desirable; sin seduces me through the commandment. Cannot adolescent sins against the flesh be explained in this way, not so much by the seductions of the flesh itself, as by this impulse towards

[4] Dr. Charles Odier, *Les deux sources, consciente et inconsciente, de la vie morale,* Ed. de la Baconnière, Neuchâtel, 1943; V. Vergriete, "La pseudo-morale inconsciente," in *Supplément de la Vie Spirituelle* (15 novembre, 1948); Dr. Georges Parcheminey, "Morales du Bien, du Devoir, et leurs relations instinctuelles," in *Psyché* (avril-mai, 1948).

14

maturity and autonomy which only a positive love for chastity could have resolved without sin and without psychic traumatism? What is forbidden incites to revolt. Is not immorality—from the most common crisis of adolescence to the Nietzschean fury—first a revolt and a non-conformity in search of life and truth? When this revolt does not succeed in freeing itself from this moral pseudo-obligation, it nourishes in the very depths of the subject a morbid anxiety and guilt. "Commandments of God, you made my soul ache," André Gide cried. That is what God's love would not have done.

When psychology and the circumstances in which the adolescent struggles make him avoid this total or partial revolt (and the masochistic guilt which ensues), he sinks into discouragement. In spite of all his efforts, he does not succeed in his first attempt to transform his life according to the absolute demands of a moral law which supposes the "acquired perfection" of him who submits to it. The adolescent despairs, renounces any moral ideal, or compromises with his conscience. It is by a laudable desire for sincerity that he ceases any religious practice: it is too hard for him. Some even come to "lose their faith."

As for those who succeed in practising the moral law, they lack the ease, the joy, the freedom, the fecundity which are the fruits of virtue. Psychologically, they remain for life retarded adolescents, conformists, tame, shy, scrupulous. No wonder, then, that religion could appear to some people as the exclusive trait of children, women, and weak-hearted, unmanly men. Having not resolved from within their problems of psychological maturity and of moral regulation, these practitioners of the law often reveal a restless and anxious unconscious psychology which stems especially from the fear of their sexuality and of their affectivity; hence their repressions and sublimations which are only counterfeits of virtue; hence their magnifying of sins of the flesh which finally absorb the entire moral life and all culpability; hence their meticulous and scrupulous prescriptions which they ask from the law (or give to it if they are moralists). Above all, however, they lack the charity which Christ nonetheless took care to give us as his commandment and as the criterion of Christian life.

While they warn us of the misdeeds which ensue from a morality of the law, faith and psychological observation teach us that an authentic morality is a morality of love and liberty, of interior truth and dynamism.

It is precisely on this point that the Gospel puts the emphasis and innovates on the Decalogue, and it is what, for several centuries, we seem to have somewhat forgotten.

It is all the more opportune to stress strongly the primacy which is given to love and interiority by the morality of the New Testament since many people today seem hardly to possess that sense of duty and law which made the greatness and the weakness of the generations before us. Gidean sincerity and Sartrian liberty—and indeed many other factors—have removed all prestige and attractiveness from the Kantian imperative. A morality of duty and law is no longer psychologically in a position to regulate our behavior. A morality of love, freedom, and interior truth has a greater chance of being accepted and proving efficient.

But then, is this not the morality of the Gospel?

There is great danger—and this can be observed even now—of not leaving room for the law under the pretext that the Christian is free, emancipated from the law (Rom. 7, 6) and living according to the inspiration of the Spirit.

Most certainly, Christian perfection is nothing else than a love, a love of God and neighbor, but this love is imposed: it is the first (and the second which is similar to it) of the commandments. We touch here upon one of the deepest paradoxes of the New Testament, for love cannot be commanded, it is inspired, and nevertheless God himself gives us the order to love: *you shall love* . . . *We must love.* That which in us is the most free, the most spontaneous, the most refractory to duty is for us a duty.

If it can be so, the reason obviously is that this commandment is not, on God's part and in regard to what we are, an arbitrary edict against nature. To love God and our brothers is indeed the law of our life, of its harmony, of its full development; but if God makes it an obligation for us, it is not only because it is necessary to our blindness and to our cowardice, it is even more (think of the first sin of humanity) because this obedience is necessary and useful to us in order to recognize, with the impulse of love, the supreme sovereignty of God over us.

The man who sins destroys himself for he fails to follow his inner law; but this would be only a prejudicial error. While deceiving himself about himself, man disobeys God: it is only to the extent that he does so that he sins.[5] To love God and our brothers is to obey our law, that of reasonable beings raised to divine life; it is at the same time to obey God. Christ—and the Christians following him—love the Father through obedience and obey him through love.[6] These two attitudes are actually one. The love of God and of one's brothers is indeed a commandment; it is *the* commandment. The virtues of charity and religion cannot be separated.

However, we do not have only the commandment to love. This love—free and obligatory—entails its obligations. This love has its precepts. "If you love me, you will keep my commandments" (Jn. 14, 15). To love Christ is to enter a network of precepts and to observe them carefully. To observe them is still to love God; for it is God, and God loved us as our Father, whom we obey by observing the commandments of his Son: "If you keep my commandments, you will abide in my love" (Jn. 15, 10). "He who has my commandments and keeps them, he it is who loves me; and he who loves me will be loved by my Father, and I will love him" (Jn. 14, 21).

Christian life and morality are, therefore, based on a commandment, to love, but they cannot exempt themselves from other commandments, which are indeed secondary and in the service of the first, but which are nonetheless commandments. "And this is love, that we follow his commandments" (2 Jn. 6).

These commandments are not only in the Gospel: to love Christ and to obey him is to belong to his mystical body, to the Church

[5] St. Thomas Aquinas, *Summa Theologica*, Benziger Brothers, Inc., 3 vols., New York, 1947; Ia IIae 21 and 71. It is necessary to have faith to understand that sin is essentially an offense to God; this is, for example, what Alexis Carrel did not understand, even though he was obviously attracted to Christianity; he writes: "Sin is the refusal to obey the order of things. All act or thought which tends to diminish, disintegrate, ruin life in its specifically human expression, is a sin" (*Réflexions sur la conduite de la vie*, Plon, 1950, p. 103); it is true that through sinning we act against ourselves, but this is exactly what offends God: "God is only offended by us through the fact that we act against our good" (*S.G.G.*, 3, 122).

[6] "For the same reason Christ suffered out of charity and out of obedience; because He fulfilled even the precepts of charity out of obedience only; and was obedient out of love, to the Father's command" (IIIa 47, 2). See IIa IIae 104, 3; IIa IIae 24, 12.

which, being as human and divine as he was fully man and fully God, cannot think of freeing herself, on this earth, of the very human laws of any society and of any psychology. Sociologically and psychologically, law is also necessary.

For this reason, it is not enough to place the love of God and of one's brothers in its right position—the very first—in Catholic morality. We must at the same time stress the necessity and the fecundity of the moral law: it is indeed the pedagogue of love and the remedy for our misery.

Certainly, there is no moral law without a love which animates it and fecundates it, but there is no morality either without a law which educates, controls, and exercises love, and which gives to it in a way the material for its development. As charity grows in us, law becomes less necessary; it will cease to be necessary only on the day of the parousia when only charity will remain and govern supremely.[7]

Sociologically, psychologically, pedagogically, the imperative constraint of the moral law is necessary to us. It is true that law is exterior to us, but the interior dynamism of love—which is itself imperative—needs this help in order to awaken, to grow, to strengthen, to secure itself against its weaknesses and its impurities, and to place itself successfully in the social body which is the Church of Christ.

The whole problem is that law *be truly in the service of love.* Or, to speak the language of psychoanalysts, the issue is for the "superego," which is necessary for the psychological growth of the child, to be balanced and little by little assumed by the dynamism of a conscious, oblatory, and free love.

It remains that Christian morality is a morality of love, which alone can make us grow in the truth of our vocation. By "speaking the truth in love," St. Paul says, "we are to grow up in every way into him who is the head, into Christ" (Eph. 4, 15).

This authentic Christian morality is not often taught nowadays in all its richness and balance. We have said enough about the unfortunate effects of this situation for them to be evaluated. It seemed opportune at the beginning of this study on affective life,

[7] Y. Congar, "La théologie du dimanche," in *Le Jour du Seigneur,* Robert Laffont, 1948, pp. 168–173.

18

conceived as the very material of morality, to situate law and love in Catholic morality, the rule of which St. John gave us in three verses of his first letter:

And by this we may be sure that we know him, if we keep his commandments. . . . For this is the love of God, that we keep his commandments. And his commandments are not burdensome. For whatever is born of God overcomes the world; and this is the victory that overcomes the world, our faith [2, 3; 5, 3–4].

Part One

A Morality of Affectivity

I.

The Moral Act
Morality and the Unconscious

It is much easier to rejoice at the sight of psychiatrists posing questions to theologians than for the theologian to give a complete and satisfactory answer in a few pages. It is deemed desirable, nevertheless, to propose here a token reply, which would have the advantage of going to the heart of the questions posed and, perhaps, offer a general principle of solution.

What is common and fundamental to all the questions raised could be formulated in these words: Does an authentic morality exist—which would presuppose moral conscience, freedom, responsibility, mind—or, after all, are what we call spiritual values (art, morality, religion) only the effects of psychophysiological determination or end-products of sublimated unconscious impulses?

This is not a new problem which, in the name of an absolute materialism and determinism, questions the existence of mind and freedom. For lack of space, and perhaps of competence, we shall limit ourselves to stating the question in a Freudian context, for it was Freud who sharpened the issue to a new edge. If conscience is only the Freudian superego, there is no such thing as moral conscience in the theological sense of the term. If religion is nothing but an obsessional neurosis, there is really no such thing as religion. Moralists are simply either great dupes or hypocrites. All man's striving for moral beauty is illusory, ineffectual, and neurotic.

To many these seem the inescapable consequences of Freudianism taken as a therapeutic method or, at the very least, as a metaphysical doctrine.[1] However, Dr. Charles Odier,[2] keeping within the limits of clinical observation, has with important insight shown that the morality of super-ego is only a pseudo-morality. He has rightly distinguished it from the "conscious morality" governed by such values as duty, goodness, mind. Other psychoanalysts also have striven to make room for spiritual values.[3] As diverse and more or less successful as these attempts have been, they all evince a start on a line of inquiry which encourages the hope that psychoanalytic doctrine and therapy will more and more take into account the features of human conduct that reveal the existence of a genuine morality.

The moral theology inspired by St. Thomas might effectively contribute to the effort so forcefully launched by Odier on the level of psychoanalysis. It is with this in mind that we would outline the structure of the moral act according to St. Thomas. After examining the essence of the moral act—its specific qualities, its sphere of influence, and its inferior analogues[4]— it will be seen how the theologian, in reference to Freud's viewpoint and particular contribution, is in a position to locate genuine moral life in its own proper domain.

1. A MORALITY OF DUTY OR A MORALITY OF HUMAN ACTS?

St. Thomas's idea of what constitutes morality is far removed from what the man in the street understands by morality in our day; and not only the man in the street, but also the majority of philosophers, moralists, and psychoanalysts! Each, though in his own particular way, sets the notions of duty and law at the center of morality.

This is not so with St. Thomas. What we call morality (the term

[1] See Roland Dalbiez, *La méthode psychanalytique et la doctrine freudienne*, Desclée de Brouwer, Paris.

[2] See Odier, *Les deux sources, consciente et inconsciente, de la vie morale*.

[3] See the works of Père Mailloux, Dr. Gregory Zilboorg, Père Bruno de Jésus-Marie, P. Beirnaert, Peter A. Dempsey, Charles Baudoin, Canon Nuttin, Dr. Fluegel, Victor White, Mme. Maryse Choisy, Binswanger, Caruso, von Gagern, etc.

[4] On this word see *infra*, pp. 52–53.

is later than he and unknown to him, as is the distinction between dogmatic and moral theology),[5] is for him, according to the old schema of the Pseudo-Dionysius, the return of the creature towards God. Since the human creature has "rationality" as the mark of his specific difference—according to which he is an image of God— this return to God is accomplished by rational acts, that is to say, by those of which he is himself the internal principle, and which he makes his own because he has control over them. After devoting the first part of the Summa Theologica to God and creation, St. Thomas opens the second part with these words:

> It remains for us to treat of God's image, that is to say, man, inas-much as he is the principle of his actions as having free will and control over his actions [Prologue, Ia IIae].

Law for St. Thomas is only an exterior help which, besides its function of promoting the common good of society, is to be con-sidered as a kindly tutor who dispenses directives and sanctions with the sole purpose of bringing about the birth and growth of "the man in the child."[6] Such a guide works from without, to awaken the child to himself, to his maturity, to his autonomy.[7]

The external law is at the service of the internal law of man's development, the law of his nature. Endowed with reason, the human creature is incited to follow the law of his nature when he discovers it within himself by the light of his reason. For a reason-able creature, to live according to the natural law is to live reason-ably. Primary and fundamental moral obligation is not imperative in the Stoic or Kantian way; nor is it of external origin as is social pressure or the Freudian super-ego—it is interior. It is to man what the biological law is to the animal. Moral obligation is an interior exigency for development along the lines of what makes him specifically man. It excludes all external constraint. This obli-gation towards his own nature is at the same time, of course, an

[5] See M.-M. Labourdette, "Chronique de théologie morale," in *Revue Thomiste* (juillet-septembre, 1956), pp. 528–541.

[6] See *Summa Theologica*, Ia 2, Prologue.

[7] See St. Thomas, *In. Ethic. Nic.,* X, *lect.* 14; *Summa Theologica* Ia IIae 90, 3, ad 2; and J. Kopf, "La loi, indispensable pédagogue," in *Supplément de La Vie Spirituelle*, no. 17 (mai, 1951) pp. 185–200.

obligation towards God. But even in regard to God, or rather, especially in regard to him, the obligation rests fundamentally on the freedom of our acts. There cannot be any constraint where the matter of specifically moral acts is concerned, because the specific character of the return of a human creature to its Creator cannot be accomplished save by free acts.

To the degree to which there is compulsion, this return is not made according to the specific law of man's nature. Such a turning back to God is distorted in nature; it is ontologically and morally bad, or at the very least imperfect: it is not human.

This basic truth is apparent also on the level of grace. The new law of the Gospel, says St. Thomas, is basically "the grace of the Holy Spirit in us which is shown forth by faith that works through love."[8] As for the secondary precepts of the new law, we fulfill them "through the interior promptings of grace" (*ex interiori instinctu gratiae*), and therefore "freely."[9]

To sum up: For St. Thomas, moral obligation consists in the fact that man, of himself, freely obligates himself to return to God according to the inward truth by which he is what he is, in virtue of his nature and in virtue of God's grace. Once this point is grasped, it is easy to understand why, in St. Thomas's treatise on the return of man to his Creator, so little space is given to exterior law. The essential part of his study bears on the acts by which man returns to God and on the principles of these acts, the virtues. St. Thomas's ethics is "dynamic,"[10] a morality of love[11] and of happiness, because it is a morality of interior liberty. It is not centered on the law or on moral conscience dictated to and pivoted on duty.

St. Thomas does not ignore conscience. He considers it an act of the intellect by which we recognize ourselves responsible for our acts, judge what we must do, accuse ourselves and experience self-reproach and remorse.[12]

[8] Ia IIae 108, 1c.   [9] Ia IIae 108, 1, ad 2.
[10] In Greek virtue is "*dynamis*"; in Latin, "*virtus*."
[11] See "Loi et Amour," in *Supplément de La Vie Spirituelle*, no. 17 (mai, 1951).
[12] "*Dicitur conscienta testifari, ligare, vel instigare et etiam accusare, vel remordere sive reprehendere*" (Ia 79, 13).

St. Thomas does not find the rule and measure of conscience in an imperative obligation, but in reason: "The rule and the measure of human acts is the reason, which is the imperative principle of human acts" (Ia IIae 9, 1).

"Obligation is a bond, not a rule," Tonneau[13] writes; and he goes on to say: "It is knowledge of the rule (or, conscience) which binds the will, and not knowledge of its obligatory character."

It was a common error in the nineteenth century to seek the first principle of moral conduct in a notion that holds true for only one topic of ethics, that of justice. It happens that the notion of duty necessarily supposes relations with others, and this notion is capable of extension only inductively (perhaps only metaphorically) to other parts of ethics, still less to the first and common principle of all moral activity.

Whether the psychoanalysts are attacking ethics or whether they are making an effort to show it some respect, it seems to us that they are mistaken when they use an ethic of duty or of obligation as their point of reference. They are excusable because it is this species of ethics that is the most prevalent even in certain Catholic circles. We consider this error to be one with very serious consequences. Odier, for example, would have given us an entirely different book and one far more enlightening for moralists and psychoanalysts both, had he been unfettered by this concept of morality.

When "the morality of conscience" is brought face to face with "the pseudo-morality of the unconscious," we find its position shifted and enhanced by a perspective unknown to the mentality inherited from the nineteenth century. If the moral life finds its first principle not in an imperative obligation, but in an inclination of nature which moves man to act according to what he is, there is a complete change of viewpoint, and, at once, the imperative drives of the super-ego show themselves in their deformities and as inadequate to animate a genuine moral life.

The comparison to be attempted here will be based on the concept of "human act" which St. Thomas identifies with moral act.

13 J. Tonneau, "Devoir et morale," in *Revue des sciences philosophiques et théologiques*, XXXVIII (avril, 1954), no. 2, p. 243.

2. THE HUMAN ACT

A. *Its Essence*

Of actions done by man, those alone are properly called *human* which are proper to man as man. Now man differs from irrational creatures in that he is master of his actions. From which fact it follows that those actions alone are properly called human of which man is the master. But it is through his reason and his will that man is master of his actions; because of this, free will is called a faculty of the will and of reason. Therefore, those actions are properly called human which proceed from a deliberate will. If there are any other actions attributed to man, they can be called acts *of man* but not properly human acts since they do not proceed from man as man [Ia IIae 1, 1; our italics].

These are the observations with which St. Thomas opens the extensive second part of the *Summa Theologica,* which treats of man's return towards God. They make very plain the fact that the return of a reasonable creature to its Creator is accomplished essentially by conjoint acts of reason and will, by free acts, in a word by "human acts." These acts are the specific object of what is now called moral theology. The moral act is the human act: "*Idem sunt actus morales et actus humani.*"[14] Any act that is not "human" has no moral value of itself.

Before going any farther, it may be well to recall what St. Thomas understands by reason, will, and freedom.

The human intelligence, first set in action by sense data, comes to know in its full capacity of certitude and clarity only after the difficult labor of abstraction and reasoning. This type of intelligence, peculiar to man, is known as reason. The will is called an "appetite," that is to say, a movement towards something else, "*motus in aliud tendens.*"[15] "The act of the will is nothing else but an inclination proceeding from an interior principle of knowledge."[16] By his rational intelligence man knows an object; he tends toward it with his will. Since love is the primary and most fundamental movement

---

[14] Ia IIae 1, 3c.   [15] *De Anima,* III, 15.
[16] Ia IIae 6, 4.

of every appetite,[17] to reduce the subject to its essential element, it can be said that to will is to love. It means loving what is known through the rational intelligence. The converse may be stated: The human intelligence is capable of an affective life proper to itself. The distinction of man from the animal does not lie solely in his speculative powers. He has also an affectivity, which can be called spiritual to distinguish it from sensible affectivity. There is in man, inasmuch as he is man, an aptitude for a mental life which too many philosophers have become accustomed to limit to philosophical or scientific knowledge. He is endowed with a power of loving which, although it is not in the sensible order, is no less (even, by that fact, better) a type of love.

Immediately, it will be apparent that St. Thomas's ethics is based entirely on the principle that the human act, that is, the moral act, is a "reasonable love." The point stressed in this statement is that an act is moral to the degree in which it is animated by love of an object known and evaluated by the rational intelligence.

At one stroke, everything that is of an arbitrary or constraining nature is eliminated from the moral act. By the act of his will, man is for himself his own principle of activity. It means that constraint on this level is a contradiction in terms. If there is coercion, there is no voluntary act, hence no moral act.[18] In the same way, if there is compulsion, there is no love. Since the moral act is an act of the will, it coincides with freedom and spiritual love. The moral act is an act of love and freedom.

Servitude is opposed to freedom. Since he who is free is his own cause [qui causa sui est], as Aristotle puts it, a slave is one who does not act as cause of his own action, but as though moved from without. Now, whoever does a thing through love, does it of himself [ex seipso operatur], because he is moved to act by his personal incentive [ex propria inclinatione]. Consequently, it is contrary to the very notion of servility to act from love" [IIa IIae 19, 4].

The moral act, then, is a "spiritual" love; otherwise, it is not a moral act. The very obligation to obey, for example, such and such

17 Ia IIae 4, 3; 36, 2; 41, 3; 70, 3. Note that St. Thomas is speaking of love not only with regard to passion, but also with regard to the rational affectivity: Ia 82, 5; Ia IIae 22, 3, ad 3.
18 Ia IIae 6, 4.

a precept, if it is to be a perfectly "moral" obligation, must be fulfilled through love and not through fear: "If you love me, you will keep my commandments" (Jn. 14, 15).

The obligation to obey a precept is not opposed to liberty except in a person whose mind is averse to that which is prescribed, as may be seen in those who keep the precepts through fear alone. But the precept of love cannot be fulfilled save by one's own will [*nisi ex propria voluntate*]. That is the reason this precept is not opposed to liberty [IIa IIae 44, 1, ad 2].

It is apparent that this conception of morality is faithful to the Gospel, which makes the whole law (and the prophets) depend on the double commandment of charity: "You shall love." It is doubtful if enough attention has been focused on the paradox involved in this commandment. Love is not something that can be commanded; a person cannot be made to love out of a sense of duty, or through coercion. This is not to say that love is not an obligation for us. There is an obligation for a child—because it is the interior law of his nature—to love his parents. He "must" love them, but if he were to love "from a sense of duty," he would not be loving them. In the same way, to perform a moral act "through a sense of duty," no matter how obligatory it may be, is to perform it in a manner which cannot be qualified as theologically moral in the perfect sense of the term. The moral act is free because it is a loving act. It is an act of love because it is free:

Since the will is ordered to that which is truly good, whenever either through passion or by a bad habit or disposition, man turns away from the true good, he acts slavishly. If the will's natural order is considered, this conduct is slavish inasmuch as man is diverted by some extraneous thing. But, from the point of view that the act of the will tends towards an apparent good (in this case, a false moral good), man acts freely when he follows passion or corrupt habit. Yet he acts slavishly if, while his will remains turned towards the false good, he refrains from what he wants from fear of the law which condemns the false good [*S.C.G.*, IV, 22, 6].

It is impossible to be more firm about excluding all servile fear from the perfect moral act. To repeat: Unless the return of the human creature to God were free, it would not be according to man's

30

nature. But it is necessary to be clear about this liberty which specifies a moral act.[19] Liberty is not contrary to necessity. St. Thomas
says: "The will desires [*appetit*] *freely,* even though it desires
[*appetat*] *necessarily.*[20] Before him, St. Augustine[21] had already
said that liberty is opposed to the necessity of constraint but it is not
opposed to natural necessity. Constraint connotes everything set up
in opposition to that towards which man tends by nature. On the
other hand, everything which corresponds to the internal law of a
being is natural to it. Every movement and every act is voluntary
which derives from the subject's own inclination.[22] Moreover, the
natural good of the will is to tend towards the good, in other words,
to want happiness. Now this willing of happiness is an act of the
will, which is to say, it is an act which has within itself its principle
of activity. Willing takes place when, of himself, man does what he
wants. Insofar as he wills, he is the principle of himself, *in quantum
est volens, principium est ex ipso;*[23] and he is master of his actions
(*dominus suorum actuum*).[24]

This is what must be labelled liberty—self-determination and
control over action. It is not opposed to any natural necessity. I
cannot will anything but happiness; it is to the degree in which I
determine myself to this act, to the degree in which I have control
over it, that there is a genuine act of the will, a human act, a moral
act.

The will in regard to perfect happiness is thus at once determined
and free. The blessed in heaven know this supreme liberty in all its
splendor; they no longer have a choice between good and evil; they
tend of themselves with their whole power of willing towards the
supreme good. They take their delight in it, and thus attain the
fullest liberty.

But, on this earth, the good appears to us and attracts us only
under multiple forms of particular goods, not one of which can fully

[19] See Jacques Maritain, *De Bergson à Thomas d'Aquin,* Hartmann,
Paris, 1957, chs. 5 and 6; also Noël Mailloux, "Determinisme psychique,
liberté et developpement de la personnalité," in *Supplément de La Vie
Spirituelle,* no. 22 (septembre, 1952), pp. 257–276.

[20] *De Potentia,* X, 2 ad 5. See Ia 82, 1.

[21] St. Augustine, *De Civitate Dei,* V, 10.

[22] Ia IIae 6, 1.   [23] IIa IIae 59, 3.

[24] Ia IIae 1, 1.

satisfy our will.[25] We must choose among these goods. Intelligence and will join forces to enlighten us about the various goods that are expedient for us under some specific aspect and make us love these goods in reference to the supreme good. It is this liberty of choice that is called free will, a joint act of reason and will.[26]

This form of liberty does not find its perfection either in the greatest possible number of objects presented to its choice, or in the greatest possible indifference in their regard, but primarily in that which constitutes the essence of liberty: self-determination. I make up my mind about such and such a choice. I make the choice my own. I commit myself to it with my whole will, which means with my love. It is in this that I am free. For this reason, St. Thomas writes that whatever we do through love, we do the most voluntarily (*Id quod ex amore facimus, maxime voluntarie facimus*[27]). It is the same case for what we do with pleasure (*ea autem quae per delectationem fiunt, sunt simpliciter voluntaria*[28]).

The more intelligent a man is, the better able he is to find a happy solution to a problem because he has an understanding of the problem. The solution thrusts itself upon him so much the more necessarily as he sees its truth. There is necessity, but no constraint whatsoever. In the same way, the more "moral" a man is, that is to say, the more deeply oriented he is towards the good and the more definitely set on his way towards it, the less is he constrained. For the moral problem posed to him, he finds the best adapted and most effective line of conduct. This line of conduct thrusts itself upon him, but without any coercion. It will be moral only inasmuch as he makes it his own, only inasmuch as he, of himself, decides on it.

The fact of being virtuous does not lessen liberty: it promotes it. This remains true even when there is no question of choice, as happens, for example, in the case of someone who has taken the three vows of religion.[29]

It thus comes about that the moral act—so aptly termed by St. Thomas the human act—has for its specific character the quality of

---

[25] Ia IIae 17, 1, ad 2; 10, 3; 13, 6; etc.

[26] Ia 82, 1–2.   [27] Ia IIae 114, 4.

[28] IIa IIae 142, 3.

[29] IIa IIae 88, 4, ad 1; 104, 2, ad 1. A slave can obey his master's orders voluntarily, that is to say, freely: IIa IIae 81, 2, ad 2.

being a self-determined act. It is of itself its own internal principle. It is free. This means that it is the product of that which specifies man as man and which usually is called his mind: rational intelligence and spiritual love.

Therefore, according to St. Thomas, morality, far from seeking its norm and perfection in law, in some superego, or in any other impulsion extrinsic to the will, takes as its norm and end the human act thus specified by liberty. The law (*nomos*) of morality is internal; it is an "auto-nomy." Every "hetero-nomy" degrades the moral act and could not constitute its essence. Just the opposite, it is the very autonomy of an act which qualifies it as moral and as principle of all morality. This characteristic furnishes the theologian with the most fundamental criterion he is obliged to use for evaluating the moral quality of any line of conduct.

B. *The Specific Qualities of the Human Act*

Essentially free, the human act is endowed with certain attributes that give it its particular character and that can serve as criteria. The following are its principal characteristics.

1. The will, therefore the human act, has for its specific object that which is known by the rational intelligence. If, on the level of essences, it is valid and useful to distinguish cognition and appetition, it is proper, on the level of operation, to study these two in their joint activity. Their collaboration is obvious in the human act, which shows the qualities of each. The will tends towards its object according to the order of reason[30]; or, which comes to the same, reason puts order into the will, order based on truth. Insofar as an object of the will is known and evaluated by the reason, it is attained in its objectivity, which means in its truth—it is known as it is. The idea which I form of it corresponds to what it is: *Adaequatio rei et intellectus.* The human act proceeds from objective knowledge. That knowledge is of the same order as scientific and philosophical knowledge. An act is neither human nor moral without this characteristic of objective truth.

2. There is a human act to the degree in which the will, the intellectual appetite, in the act itself of its affection for a particular good,

[30] Ia IIae 13, 1.

loves in the particular good a universal quality—that of goodness. "The intellectual appetite, though it tends to individual things which exist outside the soul, yet tends to them under a universal aspect, as when it desires something because it is good" (Ia 80, 2, ad 2).

To be a human act, and therefore a moral attitude, it is therefore necessary that it reach beyond the particular object loved; there must be an "open-ness" to the universal. The greater this openness, the greater is the moral value of the act. Moreover, this relationship derives logically from the concept of morality which defines it as the return of the human creature to God. In every act of intellectual cognition and of spiritual love, God is always, more or less obscurely, the object of cognition and love.[31] In fact, it is a property of man's nature to have universal ideas and to know everything under this modality. It is also a property of his will not to fix itself on that which is particular, but to go on to the universal and the unlimited. Man's will-to-be and his will-to-live, under whatever finite form they present themselves, rest on a more radical will for being and life *per se* and this is precisely the reason that concrete forms of existence never fully satisfy man. On this count, man, willing or not, loves himself in someone greater than himself, in an absolute to which he attaches his will.

By unfolding thus to God, the human act is responding as to a summons from God. Of course, it is God who allows us to posit a human act and invites us to do so. He does this by working within us, giving us that interiority of spirit which allows us to will freely, and by working from without, presenting himself to be "divined" and loved beyond the objects of our intellectual cognition and appetition.[32]

Because grace grants us the means to purify, strengthen, and raise the level of our openness to God, something that is always postulated in a human act, it has eminent moral value, the more so because it is, besides, the restoring and animating factor of our liberty.[33]

3. The human act—besides its debt to rational intelligence for these qualities of objectivity, universality, and transcendence—is

[31] Ia 12, 1; Ia 60, 5; *S.C.G.*, 3, 38. [32] Ia IIae 9, 6.
[33] Ia IIae 108, 1, ad 2; 113, 3, ad 2.

34

also under obligation to it, especially in connection with reason's practical function, for that orderly procedure whereby it goes from interior activity to exterior deployment. Ordination, the establishment of relations, is proper to reason. On the speculative plane, this function of reason is called science or philosophy. On the practical plane, it bears chiefly on relations of beings in regard to their final end,[34] *rationis est ordinare in finem.*[35]

The human act is satisfactorily oriented in reference to the authentic plenary end of man through reason. It is not the will that establishes order in the human act; the will tends towards its good according to the order of reason.[36]

4. The object of a human act has all these qualities because of the fact that it is known and evaluated by reason. It has other attributes also, derived from the will itself and the will's proper object.

The object of every appetitive faculty is the good. There is love only for what is (or seems to be) good. As intellectual appetite, the will has for object universal goodness. Of course, it tends towards individual objects, but it attains in them that which underlies all goodness. De Greeff says: "He who claims to be fighting for liberty but does not fight also for his enemy's freedom, does not fight for liberty itself but just for his own freedom." The love I bear for liberty is a human act only if it is everybody's liberty that I love in a certain person's liberty, not only and exclusively the liberty of that individual.

5. The will finds its end in this good which is loved. The end, known and willed as such, gives the human act its qualification of "human," which is the same as saying "moral."[37] The better known and willed the end is as such, the more perfectly human the act.[38] It is the quality of this end which gives to the human act its moral quality, its essence. It is a human act to the degree in which the subject orients himself, of himself and within himself, towards an end known and loved as such—in short, when there is will of an end—and the morality of the act is measured by the morality of the end.

---

34 IIa IIae 141, 6. 35 Ia IIae 90, 1.
36 Ia IIae 12, 1, ad 3, and 3, ad 2. 37 Ia IIae 1, 1 and 3.
38 Ia IIae 6, 1 and 6.

Man is able to give to himself numerous and manifold ends. There are partial or intermediate ends, there is all that is required to attain an end and that is willed in reference to it. St. Thomas says that all the last type and those *ea quae sunt ad finem* are relative to the absolute final end. This ultimate end is nothing less than the perfect good of this particular man, the good in which he finds his perfect fulfillment, which completely satisfies his intellectual appetite. Furthermore, this end can only and necessarily be one and unique.[39]

This ultimate unique end gives the human act at one and the same time its essence and its dynamism. "The principle in the successive movements of the rational appetite is the last end."[40] Any secondary good which attracts the intellectual appetite does so only by reference to the ultimate end.[41] Granted that it is not necessary for the ultimate end willed in a human act to be loved in every case by explicit, deliberate reference to that end, even so, the ultimate end must have been loved and willed in an earlier act whose orientation and intention have not been revoked but are implicitly contained in the acts which follow. The walker does not need to direct his mind at each step towards the goal of his walk; he progresses nevertheless towards it. But there must be a first step in a chosen direction and he must keep going in that direction. Man is not capable of a human act save insofar as, by a first act, he gives an ultimate end to his life. This initial moral act marks his induction into moral life. It can be understood, then, why St. Thomas asserts, in his "Treatise on Sin," that the first sin an unbaptized child can commit is never a venial sin but always a mortal sin. Before attaining the use of reason, he sins neither mortally nor venially. His first human act orders him in reference to the ultimate end of his life:

Now the first thing that occurs to a man to think about is to deliberate about himself. And if he then deliberately direct himself to his due end, he will, by means of grace, receive the remission of original sin. Whereas, if he does not direct himself to the due end, as far as

[39] Ia IIae 1, 5.   [40] Ia IIae 1, 5.
[41] Ia IIae 1, 6.

he is capable of discretion at that particular age, he will sin mortally through not doing that which is in his power to do [Ia IIae 89, 6].

This example indicates the decisive role of the ultimate end in the initial human act of moral life. It is well to notice here that the means and the objects employed to attain an end are willed only by reference, as explicitly as possible, to this end,[42] and this end is willed by reference to and because of its relation to the ultimate end. In this way, the whole voluntary movement is magnetized by the act of the will towards the final end. The better known and loved this ultimate end is as such, the more active its attractive force in the willing of secondary ends and those *ea quae sunt ad finem,* the more these subordinate ends are loved by explicit and dynamic reference to the ultimate end, the more perfect is the human act, the greater its moral value, because it means a more rapid and definite return towards God of the human creature insofar as he is human.

6. There is love and love. The love of the intellectual appetitive faculty is called "dilection." It is a love that is free and implies a choice;[43] it is the noblest type of love and the most human of the forms of love possible to man as the image of God. The moral end is thus loved with dilection. It exerts an attraction on man, it arouses and builds in him a favorable disposition towards itself, it shapes a resemblance to itself which tends towards assimilation and finally union. He who loves goes out of himself.[44] By his intelligence, man forms for himself an idea of this end; but, by love, he surrenders himself to it. Intelligence operates in an unreal and ideal mode. Love is realistic, it is *ecstatic* according to the ancients; *"oblatif,"* according to the French psychoanalysts. Therefore, one of the specific qualities of the moral act is to be ecstatic or oblatory.[45]

7. A love fulfilled is happy. It is usual to define beatitude as the perfect happiness resulting from the possession of one's last end. Here arises the old problem for which Aristotle never found a solution:[46] Is man's ultimate end beatitude or the reality itself which

[42] Ia IIae 8, 2.   [43] Ia IIae 26, 3.
[44] Ia IIae 28, 3.
[45] Ia IIae 28, 1 and 3; *Compendium Theologiae,* XLVI; *In III Sent.* 27, 1, 1.
[46] Aristotle, *Ethic.,* London, Oxford University Press, 1954, X, 6; St. Thomas, Ia IIae 4, 2.

gives beatitude? We shall give here the line of argument that St. Thomas follows in his exploration, on the plane of intellectual love, "beyond the pleasure principle."

He distinguishes, in the ultimate end of man, the end in its extra-subjective reality (*ipsa res*), and the possession of that end (*adeptio rei*). The miser's end, taken as a whole, includes the money and the possession of the money. The authentic end of man is God (*ipsa res*) and man's union with God (*adeptio rei*). This love of the *res* and of the *adeptio rei* cannot be disassociated. That does not make two ends but only one, taken in all its fullness.[47] The act and its object cannot be disassociated; they constitute a metaphysical unity.

The willing of the ultimate end, therefore, tends at one and the same time to God and to union with God. This union with God is the fruit of knowledge and of love: the vision of God effects this union, the attainment of which, fully satisfying the will, makes us blessed. The will does not seek this good to derive joy from it— that would be to put its ultimate end in its self; the *res* would not be the ultimate end. The will can be satisfied only by the goodness it finds in the object, not in itself.[48]

Knowledge from the senses, does not attain to the universal idea of the goodness common to all beings, but only to some particular good, which St. Thomas calls "delectable." Consequently, on the level of sensitive appetition, a subject acts to enjoy (*operationes quaeruntur propter delectationem*). On the contrary, the intelligence apprehends the universal concept of good—the attainment of which results in delight (*ad cujus consecutionem sequetur delectatio*) and this is why the intellectual appetite seeks the good rather than de-light[49]

In the rich complexity of the ultimate end is found a sort of hierarchy of relations. That which is willed, first of all and above all, is the end in its extrasubjective existence; then, in relation to it, the act of union with this end—the substance of this act being vision, but the act reaching its climax in enjoyment of happiness.[50] This happiness is not willed for itself as the final end; it is willed

[47] Ia IIae 11, 3, ad 3.
[49] Ia IIae 4, 2, ad 2.
[48] Ia IIae 4, 2.
[50] Ia IIae 4, 1.

only in reference to union with God, and the union is willed only in reference to God himself, and in himself.[51]

It can be seen how St. Thomas, in his concept of morality, while opening wide his arms to joy and happiness, escapes the clutches of hedonism. The "reality principle" is substituted in the human act for the "pleasure principle."[52] The Thomistic doctrine of morality neither represses nor expunges joy; it simply puts joy in its rightful place. Joy is present in the end of every human act. St. Thomas's "Treatise on Morality" begins with a study of beatitude and on that basis he constructs his whole exposition. In the opening lines of the prologue to the *Summa Theologica* (Ia-IIae, Question 6), he indicates the approach that will orient and articulate the whole second part of the *Summa Theologica*.

Since, therefore, beatitude (or perfect happiness) is to be gained by certain acts, we must in due sequence consider human acts in order to know by what acts we may obtain happiness, and by what acts we are hindered in our way to beatitude.

Beatitude, which signifies "final perfection,"[53] exercises its dynamic influence through all human acts which make us progress towards complete and final happiness. Each human act possesses also this quality of happiness, which is like "a participation in beatitude" (*ibid.*). Happiness is also its own criterion. The virtuous man acts virtuously with spiritual joy.

Since the repose of the will and every appetite in the good is pleasure, man is reckoned good or bad according to what gives pleasure to his will; since that man is good and virtuous who takes pleasure in works of virtue, and the man evil who takes pleasure in evil works [Ia IIae 34, 4].

This joy gives perfection to the human act. There is no perfectly good act without this delight in the good. So it comes about that, in a certain way, the moral goodness of this pleasure is the "cause of

---

[51] See A. Plé, "St. Thomas and the Psychology of Freud," in *Cross Currents* (Fall 1954), p. 336.

[52] This borrowing from the Freudian vocabulary does not mean, as we will show further on, that we establish an equivalence between these principles of St. Thomas and those of Freud.

[53] Ia IIae 3, 2, ad 4.

goodness in this action."[54] Joy gives the act its fulfillment *per modum finis.* To the degree that joy is integrated with the end and related to it, the will finds in it its satisfaction. Consequently, joy makes the will stronger, more persevering, and more prevalent.[55] The joy derived from the love that is called "dilection" is another specific criterion of the moral act.

8. There remains one last criterion, which is only a variant of the one above. St. Thomas labels the good which is loved in every human act, the *"bonum honestum."* A good is "useful" if desired as a means. A good is "delectable" when it is desired as bringing to the subject's appetitive faculty its repose and satisfaction. It is *"honestum"* when it is willed as the *res* which is the complete and final goal of the activity of the intellectual appetite.[56] "The useful good" is desired only by a practical reference to another good; "the delectable good" is desirable only for the enjoyment it procures. The honest good is desirable because of the goodness it[57] possesses in itself.

This does not mean that "virtuous" or "honest" good is not pleasant. Every virtuous or honest good is pleasant,[58] it is more pleasing than the "delectable good,"[59] but the pleasure it procures is not willed primarily for its own sake. What is willed is this object itself for its intrinsic goodness, for that in it which is "excellent and worthy of honor because of its spiritual beauty."[60]

The "honest good" is the specific object of intellectual appetite; the delectable good, that of sensitive appetite.[61] The human act, therefore, can be characterized by this attitude that it takes in regard to its object: a "gratuitous" attitude, one that could be called aesthetic. Goodness and beauty coincide. Though joy is not absent from the moral act, it is not sought as an end in itself—the moral act is love of the honest good.

9. It is this "honest good" which qualifies the love of friendship. According to Aristotle's well-known definition,[62] "to love is to wish

[54] Ia IIae 34, 4, ad 3.

[55] Ia IIae 33, 4, and Ia IIae 4, 1.

[56] Ia 5, 6, ad 2.

[57] Ia 5, 6, ad 2.

[58] IIa IIae 145, 3.

[59] IIa IIae 26, 12.

[60] IIa IIae 145, 3.

[61] IIa IIae 145, 3, ad 1.

[62] Aristotle, *Rhetorica,* 2, 4.

good to someone." The good thing, whatever it may be, is willed only in reference to the other's person. The love directed to that person is the love of friendship. There can be love of concupiscence in regard to things.[63] But the love of the intellectual appetite bearing upon the "honest good" has the person as term of its action. Friendship that is merely useful or pleasurable is not true friendship.[64] True friendship does not avail itself of the friend, it goes out to him not as source of usefulness or of pleasure; it is drawn to him by the goodness which he possesses. Friendship exists between one person and another (or several others). It is extended to the person himself, first of all for his good qualities, but also for all that he is, which includes even his faults.[65] Friendship is directed to the person, and even to the other persons with whom he is associated, such as his children and his friends,[66] and this love of friendship is necessarily reciprocal.[67]

C. The Human Act and the Reaches of Its Domain

It is not the hand that strikes; it is this man who is striking with his hand. It is not the intelligence that understands; it is this man who understands by means of his intellect. *Actiones sunt suppositorum.*[68] This is eminently true in the case of a human act: it is not the will that acts, it is this man willing, and doing so freely. There is a human act only if the subject, inasmuch as he is endowed with intelligence and free will, resolves of himself to posit the act.

Acts on a lower level are definitely mine. Certainly, it is I who digest, I who dream, but in themselves these acts do not involve me as a human person. By human acts alone does man act as man. Furthermore, what distinguishes him (and what at birth is only in a state of potentiality) becomes actual through these same acts. Man makes himself by undertaking human acts which, little by little as they multiply, construct the organism of virtues by which the

[63] Ia IIae 26, 4, ad 1. [64] Ia IIae 26, 4, ad 3.
[65] IIa IIae 23, 1, ad 3. [66] IIa IIae 23, 1, ad 1.
[67] *Ethic.*, VIII, 2; and St. Thomas, Ia IIae 65, 5.
[68] IIa IIae 58, 2; etc.

41

subject is more and more "disposed" to act as a human person, and by which everything in him becomes integrated.[69]

Each human act puts a little more order into the rich chaos of our personal being. This order consists in an internal harmonizing of our tendencies so that each plays its own role in harmony with the others. This can only be done if each and every tendency exercises its common finality which is to relate the subject to another being than himself, that is to say, to God.

Now if we wish to assign an end to any whole and to the parts of the whole, we shall find, first, that each and every part exists for the sake of its proper act (as the eye for the act of seeing); secondly, that less honorable parts exist for the more honorable (as the senses for the intellect); and, thirdly, that all parts are for the perfection of the whole (as the matter for the form . . .); finally, the whole man on account of his extrinsic end: possession of God.[70]

The unity of the human person, in itself and *ad extra,* is constituted, in short, by an hierarchical organization of ends. This explains the unifying and integrating role of the human act. It is essentially a love of the ultimate end; then, in the direction of the final end, of the partial ends and means adopted to reach the final end of a life specifically human. Just as the eye sees for the benefit of the whole body, the intelligence understands and the will chooses for the entire man.[71] Each appetite desires the good proper to it. Sensitive appetite seeks its pleasure, but the will must present to it a superior and ultimate end. This permits the lower appetite, while exercising always its own dynamism, to surpass itself.

It is in this way that the person finds his unity, in the object as well as in himself.[72] In this object, because, in the finanl analysis, through all the particular goods which attract him,[73] the person loves but one thing: universal transcendent goodness willed as final end. In himself, because, to the degree in which the person brings himself to will the good, it offers all the other appetites a superior end which transcends them and binds them together with harmony. It is not only the sensitive appetite which desires; the will elects this

[69] See the classical thesis on the connection of the virtues: Ia IIae 65; see also *infra,* Part Two, Chapter I, "The Virtue of Chastity."
[70] Ia 65, 2; see Ia IIae 55, 2, ad 1.   [71] Ia IIae 17, 5; 10, 1.
[72] Ia IIae 55, 1, ad 1.
[73] Ia IIae 9, 1; 73, 3, ad, 1; 114, 4.

desire and makes it its own. Thus the sensitive appetite becomes, as it were, "human." It is by this indirect process that the sphere of the passions is integrated into the person; it is incorporated by the same stroke into the moral sphere. These "humanized" passions are the objects of the virtues of temperance and fortitude.

This extension of the human act to a sphere which is, on the plane of essences, inferior to it, is termed *"imperium"* by St. Thomas. *Imperium,* by which infra-human acts are raised to the human level, is the joint operation of rational intelligence and will.[74] By that operation the sphere of human acts (therefore, of morality) is not limited to acts "elicited" by the will (that is, to those which emanate from the rational appetite as such), but reaches out to include the sensitive appetites as well. These, while of the same nature as those found among animals, transcend those of the animals by their natural capacity to lend themselves actively[75] to the *imperium* of reason and will. Thus sensitive appetites can become the principle of human acts.[76] Therefore, it is the human act which is the integrating factor in the human person.

Its extension to sensitive appetite gives the action of the will not only greater scope but greater intensity. To tend towards the good, not only by the movement of the will (prerequisite and sufficient for the act to be human),[77] but also by the movement of the passion which the will carries along and animates—this is the sign of a more intense will.[78]

By double title, then, the integration of passion with the human act makes the human act more perfect.

3. THE HUMAN ACT AND ITS INFERIOR ANALOGUES

A. Imperfect Acts of the Will

It is by a sort of participation of the lower appetite in the higher that a passion can become—as in the case of acts of temperance or fortitude—the principle of human acts.

[74] Ia IIae 17, 1.
[75] See *In III Sent.,* 23, 1, 1; *De virt. in comm.,* 4. See under "The Virtue of Chastity," *infra,* p. 125.
[76] Ia IIae 74, 3, ad 1.   [77] Ia IIae 10, 3, ad 3.
[78] Ia IIae 25, 3, ad 1; 59, 5.

When this occurs, one sees in the passions the essence and the specific qualities of the human act, which however, in virtue of *imperium,* radiate beyond the domain determined by and proper to the will. Freedom of the will is exercised in this process by taking the determinisms of the passions as material and making these determinisms its own (or by rejecting them). This potentiality of passion to be the principle of human acts leads us on a path we must now follow: the path of the participation, with its several stages, of the will act (which is the human act) in the realms of sense appetite.

With the animal, sensitive appetite tends towards objects perceived and appreciated through sense knowledge; it tends in a determined and necessary manner and not by a "free choice" (*ex judicio libero*). But, in man, this movement of the sense appetite shares in a certain way in the freedom of the will (*in hominibus aliquid libertatis participat*).[79]

A particular example will illustrate the first degree of participation of sense appetite in the will-act—"a sin of passion."[80] St. Thomas declares that there cannot be mortal sin in the order of *sensualitas.* The reason is that, for an act to be morally good or bad, it must be ordained to an end recognized as such and *sensualitas,* in itself, is incapable of effecting such a recognition. That is the prerogative of the will.[81]

A mortal sin can arise from sensuality only if the reason ordains the will to will as end the satisfaction of the movement of sensuality. In a lapidary statement, St. Thomas puts everything into place: "The cause of sin is the will (as accomplishing what gives the act its sinful character), the reason (as failing to supply to the act the direction proper to it), and the appetite (as seducing to sin)."[82]

This seduction and inclination of the sense appetite can completely blot out or partially restrict the operation of rational intelligence and will. In the second case, the human act is imperfect.[83] The proof that this act is not perfectly human lies in the fact that the will takes no joy in it; on the contrary, it is saddened: "He

[79] Ia IIae 26, 1.
[80] Ia IIae 6, 7, ad 1, ad 2; 9, 2; 10, 3; 17, 7: 74, 4; 77, 1–8; 89, 5: etc.
[81] Ia IIae 74, 4.   [82] Ia IIae 75, 3.
[83] Ia IIae 88, 2.

who sins in passion commits the sin with a certain remorse and a certain grief, while he who sins in virtue of free choice [*ex electione*] delights in the very fact that he is committing a sin."[84]

Such an act is imperfectly "human," but it remains human just the same: it is so by a sort of debased participation. This degraded type of participation would require a lengthy exposition, so it will suffice here just to cite its principal degrees.

An act, to be voluntary, must have its principle within itself and must have as object an end known and willed as such. Animals perceive an end but they do not perceive it as end; they tend towards it immediately and necessarily. Thus, they are incapable of voluntary actions in the specific and perfect meaning of the word. However, St. Thomas is following Aristotle when he says that there is something of the voluntary in the animal inasmuch as its appetite tends towards an end. This does not attest the essence of the voluntary but represents a low grade of participation in the voluntary; therefore something "imperfectly voluntary"[85] is involved.

It is the same on the plane of knowledge. What comes to us from the senses, according to St. Thomas, is endowed with a "certain imperfect [deficient] participation in intelligence."[86] This inferior participation of intelligence and will in *sensualitas* is higher in man than in the animal. It is true that the type of instinctive judgment, by which the animal gauges whether something is good for him or not, exists also in man, but with man, this instinctive judgment is enriched by a process which participates somehow in reason. In man it sets up some sort of correlations (*collationes*), not between universal ideas, as the rational intelligence would do, but between representations of concrete individual objects. "Called in animals the 'estimative' sense, the power of sensitive judgment in man is for this reason called the 'cogitative' sense or 'particular judgment.' "[87]

It is the same for memory which, in man, goes through rational and syllogistic process in recollecting the past. For this reason, St. Thomas calls the operation "reminiscence."[88]

We refer to these positions taken by Aristotelian and Thomistic

[84] In 1 Cor. 13, 2.
[85] Ia IIae 6, 2.
[86] Ia 77, 7.
[87] Ia 78, 4.
[88] Ia 78, 4.

philosophy solely for the purpose of focusing on the principle that interests us here—that of ontological participation of the lower powers in intelligence and will.

Sense knowledge in man, while remaining "animal," is experienced in a higher mode (cogitative, not estimative; reminiscence, not memory). It is the same with sense appetite.

This aptitude of sense appetite to participate in the activity of the will is a natural aptitude.[89] And this natural aptitude has degrees of explicitness and exercise, a fact which enables us to observe a full range of participation. The highest degree is attained, as already mentioned, in the acts of the virtues of temperance and fortitude, that is to say, when the concupiscible and irascible passions, participating from within, without constraint or conflict, in voluntary love, become principles of human acts.[90] As a matter of fact, in the temperate man and the man of fortitude, the passions themselves become virtues. The virtue of temperance is nothing more than a desire—in the order of passion—but a desire for what is befitting a man as such.[91] Such participation is ideal and rarely (if ever) attained, at least the stable, easy, perfectly integrated way which characterizes virtue as a *habitus*.

Be that as it may, St. Thomas, in several places in the *Summa Theologica*, marks out for observation some passions which he declares to be morally good even if they cannot be called virtues. They seek objects which are good, but in a mode imperfectly or incompletely "human." For example, it is the case of the passion of modesty and of *honestas* (self-respect), which are only incomplete virtues;[92] or other examples just as apt—pity not informed by charity,[93] contrition,[94] vindicativeness,[95] and the like. These passions, "imperfect virtues" or "seeds of virtue," are linked to temperamental traits which make a man more or less likely to be, for example, mild-

---

[89] Ia IIae 74, 3, ad 1.

[90] See *supra*, n. 75.

[91] Ia 95, 2, ad 3.

[92] See *infra*, pp. 131ff.

[93] IIa IIae 30, 3.

[94] *In III Suppl.*, 1, 2. For St. Thomas, contrition is not a distinct virtue, but the act of the virtue of penance. What is particularly to the point here is that St. Thomas recognizes the existence of "sensible" contrition which he distinguishes from "virtuous" contrition, essentially sorrow of the will. *In III Suppl.*, 3, 1; 4, 1.

[95] IIa IIae 108, 1 and 2, ad 2.

tempered or irascible.[96] It is the same case for habits and customs transmitted through family and social environment and by the laws under which one lives. The dispositions governed by all these determinants extrinsic to the will are not, in themselves, human acts, yet they can become such if the will makes them its own. Still —and this happens more readily and frequently—they may rise no higher than to a single degree of inferior participation with the will. Take, for example, any one of those passions, good in itself, which allows only the positing of an imperfectly human acts. An attitude of natural modesty is easier but less human than an act of the virtue of chastity.

B. Sub-Human Morality

In every degree of this low grade of participation in the human act one can speak of pseudo-morality or of imperfect morality, or better still, of sub-morality (as one speaks of subconscious) or, again, of pre-morality. Conduct on this level does not fulfill the requirements of the essence and specific qualities of a human act. This conduct, though, may genetically prepare the way for a human act and, when that is attained, serve as its material foundation and expression.

What are the specific qualities, what are the criteria of sub-human, or pre-human, conduct; or, to use St. Thomas's terminology, the criteria of the imperfect human act?[97]

1. This type of behavior does not have fully within itself the true principle of its activity; it is not voluntary in the sense stated above. Here we have the most specific criterion,[98] even though, in the concrete, the task of ascertaining it is not always easy—the subject's interior feeling of being free can be his own illusion.

2. The same can be said concerning the willing of the end—sub-human conduct is, indeed, directed to some definite end, but that end is not fully recognized, evaluated, and willed as such. This is especially so when it is a question of the willing of the ultimate end which presupposes, if the act is to be truly human, knowledge and love of an object, a particular one, of course, but perceived and loved in the universality and the transcendence already discussed.

[96] A. Plé, "St. Thomas and the Psychology of Freud," pp. 332–333.
[97] Ia IIae 88, 2.   [98] *De Veritate,* XXII, 4, ad 1.

47

To return to de Greeff's example: a man, unless he rises above the level of sub-human conduct, fights for his own freedom and not for his enemy's freedom also. He lives in a "closed" morality, not in an "open" one. He is not making his return to God by a specifically human route; rather, he turns back to man (individual or collective).

3. Another criterion: man's attitude when he confronts pleasure. The sensible good is the pleasurable good.[99] On the sub-human level, man acts in view of pleasure, whether it be immediate or indirect, present or delayed.[100] It has been shown that such is not the case on the plane of the human act whose specific object is the honest good.

4. The human act is not merely oblatory, it supposes friendship, which connotes reciprocity of affection between persons. Sub-human conduct is always "interested," self-seeking, even in its friendships.

5. The human act is objective. It proceeds from an objective knowledge of the object and of the means to be taken for attainment of that object. Therefore, it is precisely adapted to its end and all circumstances involved. Just the opposite, sub-human conduct derives from knowledge too rooted in the senses, only slightly disengaged from the cogitative sense and, therefore, too subjective to yield completely to reality or to pass judgment with full objectivity on the moral value of the end and its means. It adapts poorly and turns more or less completely against its objective. The sub-human act derives from an imperfect judgment of good and evil. For example, the man who has pudency will rate sins of the flesh worse than sins of the mind,[101] and, among sexual sins, will judge those more serious which are the less so, but are public.[102]

6. Even though the human act is adaptive and even, in certain cases, foreseeable, it is always original because always free. On the contrary, sub-human conduct is always more or less automatic, stereotyped, predictable, because the sensible appetite is determined to only one thing or only one line of conduct—the reverse of the human act, even when it has a passion as principle.[103]

7. Sub-human conduct proceeds less from love than from fear.

---

99 Ia 59, 4, ad 3.
101 IIa IIae 144, 2, ad 1.
103 Ia IIae 50, 3.

100 Ia IIae 4, 2, ad 2.
102 IIa IIae 151, 4.

Thus modesty is fear rising from shame, felt especially in terms of one's surroundings. It urges concealment for a bad action.[104] This means living under a morality of social pressure, under a "closed" morality. Analogical characteristics can be found in that "good passion," the sense of honor (honestas).[105] All these behaviors, in spite of their moral goodness, have not specifically and completely moral value, inasmuch as they do not meet the essential requirements of a human act.

8. Another criterion of sub-human conduct: whereas the human act is accompanied by joy, a token of beatitude and a sign that man is fulfilling himself according to his specific nature and is well started on the right road leading to God—sub-human conduct, denoting a life on the level of passion, is accompanied by conflicts, internal struggle, sadness. The fact is that, when there is not perfect virtue (when there is not a ratifying participation with intellectual appetite rendering the passions capable of a human act), the passions, if they do submit to the will, do so with repugnance. As St. Thomas puts it, they suffer violence and the results are sadness and difficulties.[106]

9. This list of the moral inadequacies of sub-human conduct could be usefully lengthened. Especially noticeable in this conduct is the complete lack of personal integration, even a certain disintegration, as well as illusions about self brought on through a life dominated by sensitive appetite, notably by concupiscence. Before Freud, St. Thomas had pointed out that lust does not show itself at once; it makes its way slowly, trying to hide itself, to disguise itself; it creeps in sorrowfully: concupiscentia quaerit latebras et dolose subintrat.[107]

C. Pre-Human Morality

Sub-human conduct can also be called pre-human in the sense that, in the genesis of the human act, it precedes the human act and prepares it.

St. Thomas does not pay much attention to this genetic aspect of a moral act (it did not appeal to the mentality of his epoch or to earlier ones). However, he does lay down some principles which are useful.

[104] See infra, pp. 132, 166.
[106] III Sent., 23, 1, 1.
[105] See infra, pp. 133–134.
[107] IIa IIae 156, 4.

On the plane of essences, the intellectual powers (knowledge and appetite) precede the sensitive and vegetative powers in dignity.[108] From this derives their precedence as regards both final end and active principle.

Those powers of the soul which have priority in the order of perfection and nature, are the principles of others in the manner of efficient and final causes. For we see that the senses are for the intelligence and not the other way about [Ia 77, 7].

In *via generationis,* the order is reversed. The vegetative powers come before the sensitive powers; the first prepare the body for the activity of the second.[109] It is the same for the sensitive powers in relation to the intellectual powers; the former are as matter and subject of activity of the latter. What is born and grows, is the animal, later the man: "The animal is generated before the man."[110] This is the regular process of nature.[111]

It is not a case of "the greater coming from the lesser." It is in man's nature that his higher powers proceed by intermediary action of his lower powers.[112] But, from the genetic viewpoint, it can be said that the greater proceeds from the lesser in this sense, that the lesser prepares and favors the activity of the greater. We could cite here with some modifications the Gospel parable of the seed and the soil which nourishes and conditions the growth of the seed (Mt. 13, 3–8). Taking human nature, what is given at the origin is, as a whole, the seed and the soil—in proportion as the soil enriches itself, absorbs the fertilizer, the seed planted there will bud forth and grow. This does not mean the same essence for seed and soil but, in man's case, they belong to the same nature, they constitute specifically the same individual subject.

For the intellectual powers to achieve a certain perfection in their activities, it is necessary that the inferior powers have attained, beforehand, to development, if not complete, at least adequate. It is significant that St. Thomas raises this point when referring to beatitude. According to him, sensible happiness is not necessary for the ultimate beatitude of heaven; the glorified body's inferior powers

---

[108] Ia 77, 4.
[110] Ia 77, 7.
[112] Ia 77, 7, ad 2.

[109] Ia 77, 4.
[111] Ia 77, 7, ad 3.

share in the happiness of the intellectual powers by a kind of redundance of overflow.[113] But, on this earth, it is very true (as he says refuting the objector) that operation of the senses is required, not essentially but accidentally, and consequently they are necessary for the imperfect happiness possible in this life. Man advances from the perfection of the lower part of himself to the perfection of the higher.[114]

Understanding of the *via generationis* is, therefore, of prime importance in a study of the human act from the concrete, pedagogical and pastoral point of view. Moral theology should study in greatest detail the development of intellectual powers from the vegetative and sensitive powers, not only in the imperfect will act which prepares the child for his first human act, and not only this first act itself, but also the progress in virtue, thanks to which the adolescent, then the man, reaches a stable and established state of interior liberty. It is one thing to be capable of performing one's first human act; it is something else to be able to perform such an act often and consistently each time a situation calls for it. The latter ability comes from a perfection of virtue which, by the improvement it brings about in the powers, establishes a firm and stable control by rational intelligence and appetite.

Between the child's first human act and the perfection of virtue lie many intermediary situations, among which St. Thomas singles out adolescence for special attention, as the minimum age to contract marriage or enter religion. For the majority of children (even if they have achieved their first human act), control by reason and its appetite is not sufficiently established, extended and stabilized to make one master of himself and his act (to what is added his legal position as a minor), for him to be able to "bind himself" in a definitive state of life.[115] From this may be concluded that the "age of reason" stretches from the moment of the first human act to the acquisition of self-control sufficient to commit one's entire self.

Four stages can be marked off schematically for this moral growth of man.

1. In early childhood, the intelligence not being sufficiently de-

---

[113] See *infra,* p. 58.   [114] Ia IIae 3, 3, ad 1, ad 3.
[115] IIa IIae 88, 8, ad 2; 88, 9.

veloped, there is not yet any human act and, therefore, no moral life. The efforts the child makes to be well behaved are on the level of the pre-moral (of the super-ego in the Freudian hypothesis).

2. The child's development attains the level where he is capable of his first human act. For the first time, according to the capacities of his age, he discovers an ultimate and universal end in relation to which he decides by himself about his life. He crosses then the threshold of his moral life.

3. Human acts multiply and, because of this, virtuous habits come to birth and develop. He thus acquires some good "dispositions" which orient him in a steady manner towards his final end. His capacity for performing more and more perfect—which means more and more free—human acts grows. But he has not yet attained to the perfection of virtue. He has, for example, attained the virtue of continence, but his virtue of chastity is still imperfect. His will is well oriented towards the ultimate end that befits him, but still feebly. His passions are not integrated by the will. In some circumstances, reason and will are dominated by his life of passion; in others they dominate it. He is divided.[116] He has an authentic moral life but he is not yet completely detached from his sub-moral life. His daily conduct proceeds from a variable combination of infantile and adult morality, sub-human morality and morality properly human. As will be indicated later, it is echoing St. Thomas to say that the majority of men tarry at this intermediary, confused stage.

4. The virtues have fully developed to form an organized whole. Man is always ready to act as befits man. He possesses on a firm, stable basis a control over his actions which extends to every possible field of activity. Here is the summit of the *via generationis* in the moral life by which man, according to that which distinguishes his specific nature, makes his return to his Creator.

D. *The Human Act and Its Inferior Analogues*

Returning to the plane of essences, it is well to have recourse to an extremely useful concept from metaphysics so as to understand the human act and assign it the proper place in relation to sub-human behaviors. The notion suggested is that of analogy.

[116] Ia IIae 10, 3, ad 2.

Applying it here, we have only to fall back on a very apt lead from Charles-Henri Nodet, who in 1948[117] proposed the same notion to clarify the so-called moral behavior of the child throughout the different stages of growth until maturity is reached. The same approach has been used by the Irish Capuchin Peter Dempsey in his recent work,[118] where he proposes the use of an analogic notion of love (from the libido to the pure love of charity).

A metaphysical analogy is valid when the same word or concept can be used to designate several realities, distinct in themselves but possessing a certain similarity. An example is the concept of Being, which is validly predicated of God, man, stone. They all exist; but each exists in a different way. God's manner of existence is essentially different from that of man, which, again, is not that of stone. But there is something common to them which allows all of them to be said to exist. There is a profound difference in the very midst of what is common between them: there is analogy. Each can be called an "analogue," God being the supreme analogue (the concept of Being verified in him to an eminent degree) and men and stones only inferior analogues because they share in Being in a definitely lower manner.[119]

For our present purpose, this concept of analogy is qualified to denote what is essentially different yet at the same time common between the "superior analogue"—the human act strictly speaking —and those more or less degraded participations which we have mentioned in sub-human or pre-human behaviors. Everything falls into place, at least speculatively, if these last two are classified as inferior analogues of the human act.

4. Towards Moral Maturity

Locating these analogues on the plane of essences has its existential correlate: not only does the human act free itself little by little, genetically, from pre-human acts, but also and above all it is proper

[117] Charles-Henri Nodet, "Vie affective infantile et vie morale adulte, notions analogues," *Supplément de La Vie Spirituelle*, no. 4 (fevrier, 1948), pp. 390–410.

[118] Peter J. A. Dempsey, *Freud, Psychoanalysis, Catholicism*, Chicago, Regnery, 1957, p. 63.

[119] H. D. Gardeil, *Initiation a la philosophie de Saint Thomas d'Aquin*, IV, 2nd ed.; Paris, Editions du Cerf, 1953, pp. 34f.

for it to make the integrating unity of all these inferior analogues which prepared its exercise.

This integration is made in time; it is an affective maturation.

This "human," and therefore moral, maturation, in fact consists in the optimum development of our spiritual affectivity, in itself and in its power to integrate the affectivity of the senses. One might well compare it to an orchestra playing with all its instruments, within the unity imposed and inspired by the composer-conductor. Without orchestra, the conductor is without means; without the conductor, there is only cacophony. Without the affectivity of the senses, man is without means; without spiritual affectivity, there is but anarchy. Maturity is the unified whole of our affectivity, our spiritual affectivity as well as the affectivity of our senses.

Finally, it is charity, "the form of all virtues," which, through its increasing control over all our acts, realizes and heightens this integration. Since charity has never ceased growing throughout our lifetime, our maturity cannot be, in every respect but above all on the Christian plane, a stable, definitively acquired and fixed state. It is by nature dynamic, evolutional, never fully and definitively resolved.

Freud is not unaware of this integration. On the level at which he places himself, he attributes its realization to the libido.[120] Eros, according to him, has as its main intention, and the ego as its main aspiration, to join, to link, to realize unity.

At the end of his life the creator of depth psychology thought that it would be better to "make our contrast not between the conscious and the unconscious but between the coherent ego and the repressed";[121] For repression, and even sublimation, have an effect of dissociation:

The super-ego arises, as we know, from an identification with the father taken as a model. Every such identification is in the nature of a desexualization or even of a sublimation. It now seems as though when a transformation of this kind takes place, an instinctual "defusion" oc-

[120] See Freud, *The Ego and the Id,* Standard Edition of the Complete Psychological Works of Sigmund Freud, London, Hogarth Press, 1961, vol. XIX, p. 45.

[121] Freud, *Beyond the Pleasure Principle,* International Psychoanalytical Library, no. 4, New York, Liveright Publishing Corporation, 1950, p. 20.

curs at the same time. After sublimation the erotic component no longer has the power to bind the whole of destructiveness that was combined with it, and this is released in the form of an inclination to aggression and destruction. This defusion would be the source of the general character of harshness and cruelty exhibited by the ideal—its dictatorial "Thou shalt."[122]

A classical example of this dissociation is given by Freud himself:

Once we have admitted the idea of a fusion of the two classes of instincts with each other, the possibility of a—more or less complete—"defusion" of them, forces itself upon us. The sadistic component of the sexual instinct would be a classical example of a serviceable instinctual fusion; and the sadism which has made itself independent as a perversion would be typical of a defusion, though not of one carried to extremes. From this point we obtain a view of a great domain of facts which has not before been considered in this light. We perceive that for purposes of discharge the instinct of destruction is habitually brought into the service of Eros; we suspect that the epileptic fit is a product and indication of an instinctual defusion; and we come to understand that instinctual defusion and the marked emergence of the death instinct call for particular consideration among the effects of some severe neuroses—for instance, the obsessional neuroses. Making a swift generalization, we might conjecture that the essence of a regression of libido (e.g., from the genital to the sadistic-anal phase) lies in a defusion of instincts, just as, conversely, the advance from the earlier phase to the definitive genital one would be conditioned by an accession of erotic components. The question also arises whether ordinary ambivalence, which is so often unusually strong in the constitutional disposition to neurosis, should not be regarded as the product of a defusion; ambivalence, however, is such a fundamental phenomenon that it more probably represents an instinctual fusion that has not been completed.[123]

On the contrary, the normal evolution of the child's development progresses towards integration:

In the process of a child's development into a mature adult there is a more and more extensive integration of his personality, a coördination of the separate instinctive feelings and desires which have grown up in him independently of one another.[124]

Complete personality is a synthesis:

[122] Freud, The Ego and the Id, p. 54.   [123] Freud, ibid., p. 41.
[124] Freud, Group Psychology and the Analysis of the Ego, New York, Liveright Publishing Company, p. 18, no. 1.

In the course of development it happens again and again that individual instincts or parts of instincts turn out to be incompatible in their aims or demands with the remaining ones, which are able to combine into the inclusive unity of the ego. The former are then split off from this unity by the process of repression, held back at lower levels of psychical development and cut off, to begin, from the possibility of satisfaction.[125]

This conception of the unity of the person,[126] by synthetic integration of the lower layers by and into the higher ones, can be found, analogically, in the Thomistic conception.

This is a general principle of the cosmos: each superior degree integrates in its being the inferior one which can then be found in it again in a more perfect form,[127] that is to say, more unitary and more simple.[128] This is a privilege of its "superiority," for the more simple a being is the more it approaches God:[129] the parts which compose it are better linked among themselves and better integrated within the subject. Its "form" more completely dominates its matter.[130]

The person is this integration of all that constitutes a man.[131] If he lacks an essential part, his body for example, he is no longer a person: after death, the separated soul is not a "person."[132]

For St. Thomas, the person is therefore the living and orderly integration of all that constitutes a man. The principle of this integration is the essential, the noblest part of man: his soul, that is, his

[125] Freud, *Beyond the Pleasure Principles*, p. 6.

[126] This conception is not found only in the depth psychology. See, for example, the works of Gordon W. Allport, and especially *Personality, a Psychical Interpretation*, London, Constable and Company, 1949. On the neurological plane, the same principle of integration is found; see Ey, *Etudes psychiatriques*, vol. I., Paris, Desclée, 1948.

[127] *De Veritate*, 14, 1; *De Anima*, II, 13; Ia 65, 2.

[128] Ia 57, 1; Ia IIae 19, 2.   [129] IIIa 6, 5, ad 2; Ia 50, 3, ad 2.

[130] *De Rat. fidei*, 6; IIa IIae 49, 6, ad 1.

[131] IIIa 2, 2. On the Thomistic concept of person, see Maritain, *The Degrees of Knowledge*, New York, Scribner's, 1959, pp. 457f.; H.-F. Dondaine, *Notes doctrinales sur la Trinité, trad. de la "Somme théologique,"* Ed. Revue des Jeunes, vol. I, pp. 237f.

[132] Ia 29, 1, ad 5; 75, 4, ad 2. Through this example one sees that the metaphysical notion of person, according to St. Thomas, is not on the same plane as the "personalistic" philosophies of today.

spiritual soul. It is in relation to it, and through the effect of its animating influence, that all the other potentialities of the person are subordinated and united to one another. Finally, the human person specifies himself through the control of his acts: he is not only "acted" upon by exterior causes, he acts by and through himself, and it is then that he posits a "human act."[133] He is free.

On the level of operation, the human person thus constitutes himself through an integration of his whole being and the effect of free acts.[134]

These human acts not only take place on the higher and specifically spiritual plane: they reach also the lower ones. If they can do so it is because these lower faculties already participate ontologically in the higher.

Generally speaking, this participation can be considered either on the ontological level where all faculties are rooted in the same person, or on the level of the action of the highest faculty upon the inferior ones.

On the former level, there is what St. Thomas calls the "redundantia."[135] It can be compared to what contemporary psychology calls the law of the economy of psychic energy: an intense act captures the totality of the subject's energy, thus polarizing around itself some of the subject's virtualities, and impoverishing or hindering all the others.

St. Thomas knows these two possibilities: impoverishment or hindrance,[136] and enrichment. He points out that passion sharpens sensory perception[137] and that spiritual joy is reflected in sensible joy. One cannot love spiritual goods strongly unless passion is involved too.[138]

Inversely, it sometimes happens that passion induces the will to

133 Ia 29, 1, and Ia IIae 1.
134 See on this subject the scholastic thesis of Cyrinus Scharf, L'habitus, principe de simplicité et d'unité, dans la vie spirituelle, Utrecht, L. V. Dekker et Van de Legt, 1950. See Dom de Roton, Les habitus. Leur caractère spirituel, Paris, Labergerie.
135 See Louis Jugnet, "L'idée de Redundantia," in La Pensée catholique, no. 13 (1950), Paris, Editions du Cédre.
136 Ia IIae 77, 1.
137 Ia IIae 80, 2; In Arist. De Somno et Vigilantia, 2, fine.
138 Ia IIae 30, 1, ad 1; 59, 5; De Veritate, 26, 7.

follow it;[139] the *redundantia* is then inverted: there is moral and psychological disorder.

On the plane of operation, this *redundantia* exercises itself by the *imperium* of the will, that is to say by the radiance, the dominating attraction, the contagion of love of spiritual appetite upon the animal appetite.[140] The mind of man has by nature what is necessary to exercise this domination which is in the last analysis nothing but the completed animation of the body by the human soul.

Let us point out once more that animation does not mean annihilation. Passions are necessary to virtue as tools are to the workman; if the sensible appetite has some defect (in terms of its order), the "imperated" act would not be perfect even if the spiritual appetite, for its part, were perfect and exercised its control over passion.[141]

If man desires as an animal and not as a man, he is not truly virtuous, even if he refuses to satisfy this desire: this refusal could be due only to his "natural dispositions" or to habit.[142] "If the matter be correctly considered," St. Thomas says, "the virtue of the appetitive part is nothing other than a certain disposition of "form" *stamped* and *impressed* in the appetitive power by reason;"[143] it is from within themselves that the inferior powers are attracted towards the objects of the superior power; owing to which the very root of the disorder pertaining to passions is extirpated.[144] It is only then that man is perfect, for all his faculties can operate harmoniously, without opposing or destroying one another, as can be seen especially in the human life of Christ.[145]

The difficulty comes from the fact that animal joys are felt more strongly than spiritual joys.[146] This cannot surprise a depth psychologist: in an analogous way, Freud finds the same law at the lowest levels of the psyche and its integration:

[139] Ia IIae 9, 2; 10, 3; 77, 1, 2, and 6.

[140] See *infra,* pp. 127–128.

[141] IIa IIae 141, 1, ad 2.

[142] IIa IIae 141, 1, ad 2. St. Thomas knows too the "pseudo-morality."

[143] *De Virtute in comm.,* 9.

[144] See, for example, Ia IIae 66, 4, ad 2.

[145] IIIa 15, 9, ad 3.

[146] Ia IIae 31, 5, ad 1; IIa IIae 141, 4, ad 4. That is why most men are hardly sensible but to the lower joys: IIa IIae 35, 4, ad 2.

And there seems to be no doubt whatever that the unbound or primary processes give rise to far more intense feelings in both directions (pleasure and unpleasure) than the bound or secondary ones.[147]

. This weakening of feeling is really due to integration:

Our experiences have taught us with certainty that the mental and somatic power of a wishful impulse . . . is far stronger if it is unconscious than if it is conscious. . . . An unconscious wish cannot be influenced and it is independent of any contrary tendencies, whereas a conscious one is inhibited by whatever else is conscious and opposed to it.[148]

But if the most inferior desires are more vehement when they are left to themselves, their integration by the mind must, in the end, give them all their acuteness. He who is temperate appreciates, all the better, the delicacies and joys of eating.

We can thus see the great extent to which, according to the Thomistic conception, the animal receives a renewal of vitality and nobleness from its integration with mind. The law of the human person is to thus integrate all that constitutes him in the mind. A Thomist can but subscribe to affirmations like Odier's:

The primary condition for balance between will and senses, between ideal and instinct, is knowledge. Knowledge conditions and rules the secondary action of *the principles of coincidence and prevalence*.

To formulate such principles finally comes down to defining the Apollinian type dear to Goethe in which "the ideal of the person is realized when a high degree of spiritual evolution is based on powerful vital foundations," as Thibon has said so well. But this is true, we must add, only if these foundations can be the object of knowledge and of clear discrimination, and not of confusion with repressed vital tendencies.[149]

For St. Thomas, the strictly spiritual activities have too their exigencies, their laws of integration into the human person. The virtuous *"habitus"*[150] not only perfect powers, they enable them to

[147] Freud, *Beyond the Pleasure Principle*, p. 86.
[148] Freud, *Five Lectures on Psychoanalysis*, Standard Edition, vol. XI, p. 53.
[149] Odier, *Les deux sources, consciente et inconsciente, de la vie morale*, p. 177.
[150] See *infra*, p. 179.

be better harmonized and better integrated into the person. As the eye sees for the whole body, intelligence understands for all the spiritual powers.[151] Not only can the same virtue perfect several powers and make them act in unity,[152] but several virtues can unite and subordinate themselves to one another in the unity of one and the same act,[153] as is the case, in particular, for the free act which proceeds from the joint action of intelligence and will.

By *redundantia* and by their reciprocal action, virtues are connected with one another:[154] one has either all of them or none.[155] Natural virtues are connected to one another by prudence; on the supernatural plane, it is charity which, animating them by its object, ties all the virtues, natural and supernatural, together and gives them their perfection.[156] Virtues are even connected in their growth: they grow, according to the image given by St. Thomas, like the fingers of the hand.[157]

Inversely, vices are not connected.[158] They no doubt engender one another—and this is why they are called capital[159]—but they do so in the manner of a chain disintegation of atoms: they dissociate the human person, aggravating the natural contradiction which man finds in himself between spirit and matter—a contradiction caused by original sin[160] and which sanctifying grace heals and raises.[161]

The virtuous man loves a unique good and all others only in reference to this ultimate end: he finds in it his unity. The vicious man inclines towards goods which are not only false, but multiple and contradictory;[162] he dissociates himself in them.

This moral disintegration, or abortive integration of the person, has for matter and consequence a psychic disintegration of the human person. Sin is, in short, a psychological dissociation, which

---

[151] Ia IIae 17, 5, ad 2.   [152] Ia IIae 56, 2.
[153] See Ia IIae 13, 1; 14, 1, ad 1; 17, 1 and 4; 18, 6; etc.
[154] Ia IIae 61, 4, ad 1.   [155] Ia IIae 65.
[156] Ia IIae 65, 2; and IIa IIae 23, 7 and 8.
[157] Ia IIae 66, 2.   [158] Ia IIae 73, 1.
[159] Ia IIae 84, 3.   [160] Ia IIae 82, 2.
[161] Ia IIae 82, 3; *De Veritate*, 25, 6; *S.C.G.*, 4, 1; *Questio unica de Anima*, 8, 7. Grace, however, does not totally cure the disorder of original sin: *S.C.G.*, 4, 52.
[162] Ia IIae 73, 1.

is sin only insofar as it is a conscious and free offense to the law of God. Even if sin is only material, that is to say, if the circumstances in which it has been committed do not entail any moral culpability, it remains dissociative of the person. The moralist must not forget this and must not limit his study of sin to culpability.

For psychoanalysis, this distintegration is called neurosis and, in the most serious cases, psychosis. *Analogically,* the process is the same as for sin: it is a disintegration.[163] As a matter of fact, Freud writes:

Even in organisms which later develop an efficient ego-organization, their ego is feeble and little differentiated from their id[164] to begin with, during their first years of childhood. Imagine now what will happen if this powerless ego experiences an instinctual demand from the id which it would already like to resist (because it senses that to satisfy it is dangerous and would conjure up a traumatic situation, a collision with the external world) but which it cannot control, because it does not yet possess enough strength to do so. In such a case the ego treats the instinctual danger as if it were an external one; it makes an attempt at flight, draws back from this portion of the id and leaves it to its fate, after withholding from it all the contributions which it usually makes to instinctual impulses. The ego, as we put it, institutes a *repression* of these instinctual impulses. For the moment this has the effect of fending off the danger; but one cannot confuse the inside and the outside with impunity. One cannot run away from oneself. In repression the ego is following the pleasure principle, which it is usually in the habit of correcting; and it is bound to suffer damage in revenge. This lies in the ego's having permanently narrowed its sphere of influence. The repressed instinctual impulse is now isolated, left to itself, inaccessible, but also uninfluenceable. It goes its own way. Even later, as a rule, when the ego has grown stronger, it still cannot lift the repression; its synthesis is impaired, a part of the id remains forbidden ground to the ego. Nor does the isolated instinctual impulse remain idle; it understands how to make up for being denied normal satisfaction; it produces psychical derivatives which take its place; it links

163 It would be most interesting to be able to specify the differences which make the forms of psychological disintegration absolutely distinct from that of sin. It would also be necessary to look for the resemblances and the dependencies. One can here only mention the interest of such a work.

164 On the "id," see *infra,* n. 173.

itself to other processes which by its influence it likewise tears away from the ego; and finally it breaks through into the ego and into consciousness in the form of an unrecognizably distorted substitute, and creates what we call a symptom. All at once the nature of a neurotic disorder becomes clear to us: on the one hand an ego which is inhibited in its synthesis, which has no influence on parts of the id, which must renounce some of its activities in order to avoid a fresh collision with what has been repressed, and which exhausts itself in what are for the most part vain acts of defence against the symptoms, the derivatives of the repressed impulses; and on the other hand an id in which individual instincts have made themselves independent, pursue their aims regardless of the interests of the person as a whole and henceforth obey the laws only of the primitive psychology that rules in the depths of the id. If we survey the whole situation we arrive at a simple formula for the origin of a neurosis: the ego has made an attempt to suppress certain portions of the id *in an inappropriate manner,* this attempt has failed and the id has taken its revenge. A neurosis is thus the result of a conflict between the ego and the id, upon which the ego has embarked because, as careful investigation shows, it wishes at all costs to retain its adaptability in relation to the real external world. The disagreement is between the external world and the id; and it is because the ego, loyal to its inmost nature, takes sides with the external world that it becomes involved in a conflict with its id. But please observe that what creates the determinant for the illness is not the fact of this conflict—for disagreements of this kind between reality and the id are unavoidable and it is one of the ego's standing tasks to mediate in them—but the circumstance that the ego has made use of the inefficient instrument of repression for dealing with the conflict. But this in turn is due to the fact that the ego, at the time at which it was set the task, was undeveloped and powerless. The decisive repressions all take place in early childhood.[165]

One will have noted that in this long passage repression is in fact considered as an abortive integration. Psychoanalytic treatment has the effect of liberating the unconscious desires which have escaped the synthesis of the ego; they can then be integrated into it by different processes which Freud enumerates:

[165] Freud, *The Question of Lay Analysis,* Standard Edition, vol. XX, pp. 202–204.

The most frequent outcome is that, while the work is actually going on, these wishes are destroyed by the rational mental activity. . . . Repression is replaced by a condemning judgment carried out along the best lines. That is possible because what we have to get rid of is to a great extent only the consequences arising from earlier stages of the ego's development. The subject only succeeded in the past in repressing the unserviceable instinct because he himself was at that time still imperfectly organized and feeble. In his present-day maturity and strength, he will perhaps be able to master what is hostile to him with complete success.

A second outcome of the work of psychoanalysis is that it then becomes possible for the unconscious instincts revealed by it to be employed for the useful purposes which they would have found earlier if development had not been interrupted. For the extirpation of the infantile wishful impulses is by no means the ideal aim of development. Owing to their repressions, neurotics have sacrificed many sources of mental energy whose contributions would have been of great value in the formation of their character and in their activity in life. We know of a far more expedient process of development, called *"sublimation,"* in which the energy of the infantile wishful impulses is not cut off but remains ready for use—the unserviceable aim of the various impulses being replaced by one that is higher, and perhaps no longer sexual. It happens to be precisely the components of the sexual instinct that are specially marked by a capacity of this kind for sublimation, for exchanging their sexual aim for another one which is comparatively remote and socially valuable. It is probable that we owe our highest cultural successes to the contributions of energy made in this way to our mental functions.[166]

One of Freud's most serious lacunae is scarcely to have studied processes of integration other than sublimation. Sublimation, for the impulses, is like an *unconscious* displacement of their objects: these impulses, unable to exercise themselves freely, succeed in finding *of themselves* an outlet towards an object completely different from their own. Sexual impulses, for example, when they cannot be satisfied by their object, sublimate themselves and incline towards art or religion.

Freud himself seems to recognize that sublimation goes hand in

[166] Freud, *Five Lectures in Psychoanalysis,* Standard Edition, vol. XI, p. 53.

hand with a certain dissociation;[167] in the passage just cited above, he speaks of the enrichment which *follows* sublimation. What does he mean by this? In any case, one could not admit that of itself sublimation provides the true integration of the person.

We would be inclined to think that the authentic and full integration of the human person—inasmuch as it is specifically human—, even if it is preceded by sublimation (which is already acquired by the "age of reason"), and even if it finds support in it, has a very different structure. Complete and successful integration is like an "assumption" exercised by the higher level of our psyche with respect to the lower ones. It is not the lower levels which of themselves find an outlet in the higher level: it is the higher level which attracts to itself the lower ones, coordinates them, unifies them *from above,* and makes them participate in its nobleness.

Sublimation is an unconscious process. How could one maintain that the unity of man is realized but unconsciously? The assumption is by definition conscious: it is a sort of radiation of psychological consciousness and moral conscience on all of our being.[168]

It is difficult to see what would keep psychologists from studying the conscious process of the integration of the person. They could but profit themselves by it. And moralists would receive from them a more extensive knowledge of the psychological laws of the moral integration of the human person.

5. MATURITY AND SPIRITUAL CHILDHOOD

This complete integration of the person, the fruit of psychic and moral maturity, knows by the action of God's grace a transcendence which is at the same time a reversion. Full Christian maturity is fulfilled in what is generally called spiritual childhood.

As a matter of fact, this maturity is that of a child (of God). And the spirit of childhood, which is the opposite of infantilism, seems to me to crown any genuine Christian maturity. This truth is

---

[167] See Freud's passage which we have quoted, *supra,* pp. 54–55.

[168] This distinction between Freudian sublimation and what we call "assumption" has not been sufficiently emphasized by Konstanty Michalski, in his study "La sublimation thomiste," in *Angelicum* (janvier, 1937), pp. 212–222.

paradoxical in appearance only and one can reach some understanding of it.

Odier, extending Piaget's thought in the light of Freud, defines the last stages from adolescence (ages twelve to twenty) to maturity. "It consists," he says, "in passing healthily from affective realism to the acquisition and preservation of the sense of internal security (the process of endogenous security or *securization*), to the sense of internal self-value (the process of endogenous *valorization*), to the sense of autonomy (the process of endogenous *autonomization*)."[169] By their increasing activity, virtues—the capacities to posit human acts and to thus progress towards beatitude—place us indeed in this state of security, "*valorization*," and autonomy. But the theological virtues and their acts transcend, super-achieve, and in a way reverse this human maturity. Indeed by faith, hope, and charity, and by the gifts of the Holy Spirit, the Christian lives in a super-human security. His Father is God, what could he fear? He knows (by faith) that he has an infinite value, for the only begotten Son of the Father died and rose again for him; he who is Love itself loves him, and with a gratuitous, gracious, eternal love always present and active in his life. As for his freedom, the gift of God restores it in him. The grace of God, precisely because it comes from God, is endogenous and has a depth which we cannot suspect. It permits us to act on a level of interiority and of personal self-determination which the sinner cannot reach.

Thus the affective maturity of the Christian blossoms in spiritual childhood, which is only, in short, a supermaturity wrought by grace.

In a word, for the theologian, affective maturation is none other than progress towards human divine perfection. It is an unceasing movement of actuation of that which is specific in man, whom grace transforms into a son of God. This movement begins on the biological plane, then on the psychological level, then ascends to the human act, then to virtues. In the Christian, present grace, since his baptism, progressively exercises this power of integration in order to make of the completed man a son of God. Though distinct in

[169] Odier, *Anxiety and Magic Thinking*, New York, International Universities Press, 1956, p. 24.

their essence, these stages are one in the existential development of the person in the process of acquiring his maturity.

6. Sub-Human Lines of Conduct

Understanding of the human act and of the sub-human or pre-human behaviors such as we have endeavored to convey, will make it possible to understand the psychology of the unconscious described and discussed by Freud and his successors—and to allot it the place it deserves.

As said above, Odier has laid down broad lines of discernment of these two sources of morality, conscious and unconscious. It would seem that St. Thomas gives a conception of morality much more favorable to this dichotomy than that derived by Odier from duty and conscience. It is not our task, since we are not psychoanalysts, to study the data reported by Odier and his analyses of these data. But the theologian, after reading Odier's study, finds himself in a position, and on solid ground, to take a stand for comparing what concerns him as moralist with what concerns the psychoanalyst.

It seems that Freud and his successors (speaking only of those in the movement of contemporary psychology and psychiatry) do not concern themselves with what we have called the human act; they concern themselves with its inferior analogues. We think that whoever reads Freud in the light of the analogy of the human act, has the criterion for discerning what is true and false in the Freudian approach. Such a reader benefits by a research hypothesis workable on the level of observation as well as of theory, which can be invoked to redirect and extend (also improve, perhaps) therapeutic technique and especially psychological theory. It is evident that Freud made no distinction between the human act and its analogues. He was almost exclusively preoccupied with the latter. But it would be oversimplifying his attitude—and perhaps falsifying it—to declare that he denied the existence of the human act. Generally, his writings are silent on this point, or, if he does speak of it, he is confused and contradictory. We shall take only a few examples.

On the one hand, he professes an unqualified determinism:

Once before I ventured to tell you that you nourish a deeply rooted faith in undetermined psychical events and in free will but that this is quite unscientific and must yield to the demand of a determinism whose rule extends over mental life.[170]

On the other hand, he speaks of freedom: "We must recognize here a degree of freedom which cannot be resolved any further by psychoanalytic means."[171]

He speaks also of self-control:

It is well known that the ideal case for an analyst is one where a client, who possesses self-control and is suffering from some interior conflict which he cannot resolve, brings his trouble to the psychoanalyst and asks his assistance.[172]

Freud grants a definite, elevated position to culture, art, even to morality and religion, the birth and development of which he attributes to the ego—and in terms which seem to befit partially what we have called the human act.

Starting from conscious perception, the ego has brought under its influence ever larger regions and ever deeper layers of the id;[173] and, in the persistence with which it maintains its dependence upon the external world, it bears the indelible stamp of its origin (as it might be "Made in Germany"). Its psychological function consists in raising the processes in the id to a higher dynamic level (perhaps by transforming freely mobile into bound energy, such as corresponds to the preconscious condition); its constructive function consists in interposing, between the demand made by an instinct and the action that satisfies it, an intellective activity which, after considering the present state of things and weighing up earlier experiences, endeavors by means of experimental actions to calculate the consequences of the proposed line of conduct. In this way the ego comes to a decision.[174]

[170] Freud, Introductory Lectures on Psychoanalysis, Standard Edition, vol. XV, p. 106. See also Freud, "Psychopathology of Everyday Life," in The Basic Writings of Sigmund Freud, New York, Random House, 1938, pp. 161f.

[171] Freud, Leonardo da Vinci, Standard Edition, vol. XI, p. 135.

[172] Freud, Collected Papers, vol. II, London, Hogarth Press, 1953, p. 205. See also Freud's text quoted on p. 63.

[173] The id ("es" in German) designates the "system of unconscious tendencies which direct, either unconsciously or against his will, the psychical activity of an individual ["id is stronger than ego"]. Tendencies or prefigurations of behavior come from the instinctual life and particularly from sexuality" (A. Hesnard, Manuel alphabétique de Psychiatrie, P.U.F., 1952).

[174] Freud, An Outline of Psychoanalysis, London, Hogarth Press, 1949, p. 69f.

Freud goes so far as to write: "The ego represents what we call reason and sanity, in contrast to the id which is dominated by the passions."[175]

He affirms that analysis is concerned with moral values:

Psychoanalysis has been reproached time after time with ignoring the higher, moral, spiritual side of human nature. The reproach is doubly unjust, both historically and methodologically. For, in the first place, we have from the very beginning attributed the function of instigating repression to the moral and aesthetic tendencies in the ego, and secondly, there has been a general refusal to recognize that psychoanalytic research could not produce a complete and finished body of doctrine, like a philosophical system, ready-made, but had to find its way step by step along the path towards understanding the intricacies of the mind by making an analytic dissection of both normal and abnormal phenomena. So long as the study of the repressed part of the mind was our task, there was no need for us to feel any agitated apprehensions about the existence of the higher side of the mental life. But now that we have embarked upon the analysis of the ego we can give an answer to all those whose moral sense has been shocked and who have complained that there must surely be a higher nature in man: "Very true," we can say, "and here we have that higher nature, in this ego-ideal or super-ego, the representative of our relation to our parents."[176]

Freud insists that the "ego-ideal answers in every way to what is expected of the higher nature of man"[177] and that the normal development of the ego goes in the direction of moral progress:

The ego develops from perceiving instincts to controlling them, from obeying instincts to curbing them. In this achievement, a large share is taken by the ego-ideal, which indeed is partly a reaction-formation against the instinctual processes in the id. Psychoanalysis is an instrument to enable the ego to push its conquest of the id further still.[178]

Freud recognizes that joy in intellectual work has a special quality which he hopes some day to be able to define:

Another method of guarding against pain is by using libido-displacements that our mental equipment permits, by which it gains so greatly

[175] Freud, *The Ego and the Id,* London, Hogarth Press, 1950, p. 30.
[176] *Ibid.,* p. 46f. On the ego and the id, see the very enlightening pages by Odier, Anxiety and Magic Thinking, pp. 32–43.
[177] *Ibid.,* p. 49.   [178] *Ibid.,* p. 82.

in flexibility. The task is then one of transferring the instinctual aims into such directions that they cannot be frustrated by the outer world. Sublimation of the instincts lends an aid in this. Its success is greatest when a man knows how to heighten sufficiently his capacity for obtaining pleasure from mental and intellectual work. Fate has little power against him there. This kind of satisfaction, such as the artist's joy in creation, in embodying his phantasies, or the scientist's in solving problems or discovering truth, has a special quality which we shall certainly one day be able to define metaphysically. Until then we can only say metaphorically it seems to us "higher and finer," but compared with that of gratifying gross primitive instincts its intensity is tempered and diffused; it does not overwhelm us physically. The weak point of this method, however, is that it is not generally applicable; it is available only to the few. It presupposes special gifts and dispositions which are not very commonly found in a sufficient degree. And even to those few it does not secure complete protection against suffering; it gives no invulnerable armour against the arrows of fate, and it usually fails when a man's own body becomes a source of suffering to him.[179]

He likewise recognizes the existence of altruistic love:

. . . we may expect that within the very period of life which we reckon as childhood, altruistic impulses and morality will awake in the little egoist, and that . . . a secondary ego will overlay and inhibit the primary ego.[180]

He enlarges the concept of libido to dimensions of love such as were taught and lived, not only by Plato, but St. Paul[181] and also St. Francis of Assisi, although he remarks that:

A small minority are enabled by their constitution nevertheless to find happiness along the path of love; but far-reaching mental transformations of the erotic function are necessary before this is possible. These people make themselves independent of their object's acquiescence by transferring the main value from the face of being loved to their own act of loving; they protect themselves against loss of it by

179 Freud, *Civilization and Its Discontents,* London, Hogarth Press, 1939, p. 33f.
180 Freud, "The Interpretation of Dreams," in *Basic Writings of Sigmund Freud,* p. 299.
181 Freud, *Group Psychology and the Analysis of the Ego,* Standard Edition, vol. XVIII, p. 91.

attaching their love not to individual objects but to all men equally, and they avoid the uncertainties and disappointments of genital love by turning away from its sexual aim and modifying the instinct into an impulse with an *inhibited aim*. The state which they induce in themselves by this process—an unchangeable, undeviating, tender attitude—has little superficial likeness to the stormy vicissitudes of genital love, from which nevertheless it is derived. It seems that Saint Francis of Assisi may have carried this method of using love to produce an inner feeling of happiness as far as anyone; what we are thus characterizing as one of the procedures by which the pleasure-principle fulfills itself has in fact been linked up in many ways with religion; the connection between them may lie in those remote regions of the mind where the distinctions between the ego and objects and between the various objects become matters of indifference. From one ethical standpoint, the deeper motivation of which will later become clear to us, this inclination towards an all-embracing love of others and of the world at large is regarded as the highest state of mind of which man is capable.[182]

The question arises whether Freud would have noticed and recognized a true human act. It is very evident that he had experienced them himself in his own life, but in his writings he scarcely mentions them unless it is to trim them down systematically to what we have called the human act's preparatory stages in the *via generationis*. Culture seems to be for him only the end-product of eros-sublimation; religion, an infantile obsessional neurosis; morality, the dissociative aggressive conflict of the super-ego with the ego. With Freud, morality seems to be only restriction of the instincts, prohibitions, categorical imperatives.[183] The ego-ideal, also, is prohibitory.[184] Since conscience is to Freud a function of the super-ego, it

[182] Freud, *Civilization and Its Discontents,* p. 69f.

[183] The reader can judge by phrases such as these: "From the point of view of morality the control and restriction of instinct, it may be said of the id that it is totally non-moral, of the ego that it strives to be moral, and of the super-ego that it can be hyper-moral. . . . But even ordinary normal morality has a harshly restraining, cruelly prohibiting quality . . . the source of the general character of harshness and cruelty exhibited by the ideal—its dictatorial 'Thou shalt' " (*The Ego and the Id,* pp. 79f.). Many other passages could be quoted where morality is presented along these lines, especially *Totem and Taboo.*

[184] "But the Ego-ideal comprises the sum of all the limitations in which the Ego has to acquiesce" (Freud, *Group Psychology and the Analysis of the Ego,* Standard Edition, vol. XVIII, p. 131.

has for him the same characteristics (restraint from without, restriction of instincts, need of punishment, etc.).[185]

This reduction process, practically constant with Freud, going from more to less, from superior to inferior, appears to us both valid and invalid. It is valid if the fact is kept in mind that Freud is a medical man looking for a therapy applicable to neurotics. From this point of view, he has a right to narrow his study to what he calls "ordinary normal morality,"[186] which means the code of the majority of people, or "what the ordinary man conceives when he speaks of religion."[187] The theologian should not forget that St. Thomas himself observed sadly, over and over again, that the majority of men live on the level of their passions; that St. Thomas states precisely that these men are puppets under the sway of cosmic forces[188] and the activity of Satan who has not the least power over human acts but influences the imagination and the sensitive appetite[189]—we would say here the sub-human conduct and the inferior analogues of the human act. Rare (*pauci, pauciores,* writes St. Thomas) are those men who raise themselves above this level.

To take a typical example: The majority of men who are commonly recognized as "moral," remaining, where matters of sexual morality are concerned, on the level of decency and *honestas,* do not rise to the regular practice of the virtue of chastity. They live thus on the plane of sub-human acts, which, of course, does not prevent them from occasionally performing a human act.

Moral theology does present, and should, the ideal standards. The physician as such, and the same for the sociologist and the ethnologist, is concerned only with observation of facts. Now it cannot be denied that usually the moral conduct of the majority of men scarcely rises above the inferior analogues of the human act. Therefore, no one has a right to blame Freud for remarking on the circumstance, and it is to be wished that moralists would face up to the incontestable evidence, while the psychoanalysts, on their part,

[185] See, for example, Freud, *Civilization and Its Discontents,* pp. 105–122.
[186] Freud, *The Ego and the Id,* p. 80.
[187] Freud, *Civilization and Its Discontents,* p. 23.
[188] Ia 115, 4, ad 3; Ia IIae 9, 5, ad 3; IIa IIae 95, 5, ad 2; *S.C.G.,* 3, 85.
[189] Ia IIae 80, 1–4; IIa IIae 95, 5; *S.C.G.,* 3, 92.

would not deny the possibility, and even the existence, of human acts.

A further point—observation essentially deals with the *via generationis* and we have seen that it can be affirmed, along with St. Thomas, that on this plane, and in a certain way, the greater derives from the lesser.

Finally, Freud was a physician of the mentally ill. With such patients, inasmuch as they are mental patients, the functioning and the sovereignty of the rational intelligence and its appetite are impaired.[190] With mental patients, even more than with the man in the street, "moral" conduct can be (to put the matter at its best) only at the level of inferior analogues of the moral act.

For all these reasons, Freud's stand seems valid to us. But it fails to be so the moment he claims to give a complete and absolutely final explanation of facts observed—in a word, as soon as he gives free rein to his tendency to philosophize, to set up a metapsychological system. To limit ourselves to just one example, we object when he writes:

If we assume as a general hypothesis that the force behind all human activities is a striving towards the two convergent aims of profit and pleasure, we must then acknowledge this as valid for other manifestations of culture.[191]

Freud is wrong when he ignores the "honest good," which, as we have seen, specifies the human act. Thus, he confines his inquiries to the realm of sub-human morality, to the domain that Bergson called the "closed morality" ("*la morale close*").

If we recall all that Freud has written depicting the evolution or involution of the ego and the super-ego (especially by reading or rereading his study entitled *The Ego and the Id*), it will be noted that, to the degree this process bears a "moral" significance, his laws have characteristics analogous to those which St. Thomas recognizes for sub-human acts. This is particularly clear-cut in regard to the imperfectly moral conduct of the (good) passion of modesty, which is specified by fear in relation to the animal appetite in man (and not by a participation of passion-love with intellectual love, which

---

[190] I–II 73, 3; etc.
[191] Freud, *Civilization and Its Discontents*, p. 57f.

defines the virtue of chastity). Also, this fear has a parental or social reference. Thus the sexual appetite is not modified from within by the "order of reason," it is not integrated to the human person in reference to what makes him human, and then this person is incapable of a human act. It is a morality of imperative and categorical interdicts. The sexual appetite suffers violence; there is conflict and sadness.[192]

It is impossible to carry out in detail here a theological interpretation of Freudian findings on the plane of the human act's inferior analogues. Within the framework of these pages, we must be satisfied with having suggested just one theological principle which permits distinction between the true and the false in the Freudian approach.

By way of conclusion and to confirm the explanatory value of the analogy-principle just proposed, we would like to point out how harmful its neglect can be, and how such neglect opens the way to statements satisfactory neither to psychoanalysis nor to moral theology.

For example, Charleen Schwartz,[193] full of good intentions in the rapport she establishes between St. Thomas and Freud, writes that "Freud's super-ego corresponds to Aristotle's practical intellect" (p. 5); that the id, in the same way, "corresponds to animal appetite" (p. 7); and the ego "to the will" (p. 7). It is true that she takes care to state that the "correspondence" here involved is not an "identity" (p. 5), but she asserts that, even though the super-ego was not considered by Freud as an "essentially rational function," it is clear that he is describing this point of morality "almost exactly as a Thomist would" (p. 6). From this she deduces that "one part [?] of the super-ego is nothing else but moral conscience" (p. 8). Consequently, for her, "it is a failure to resolve intense conflicts of conscience which leads to neurosis" (p. 9), and therefore "a healthy moral judgment is indispensable for a good psychoanalyst" (p. 12). For "the neurotic cannot be cured until he is morally strengthened to the point where he can bring his emotions under the control of

[192] *III Sent.*, 23, 1, 1.
[193] Charleen Schwartz, *Neurotic Anxiety*, New York, Sheed and Ward, 1954.

reason."[194] In the article from which the last quotation was taken, the author repeats this opinion emphatically:

Our position is that the psychiatrist cannot remove the psychological disorders without the moral reëducation of the conscious normal part of the personality, because *the emotions are inhibited in the first place due to a moral weakness, that is, the moral ego in its weakness could only inhibit the emotions as a defense against carrying them out* [*Ibid.*, p. 13; our italics].

Here there is evident confusion between the human act and its inferior analogues. This results in bad theology and bad psychology and great danger on two levels, psychoanalytical therapy and direction of conscience.

The same kind of confusion exists in the work of Wilfried Daim[195] who, as a more or less loyal disciple of Kierkegaard and Heidegger on the one hand and of Freud on the other, thinks that "it is openness [*ouverture*] to the Absolute . . . which confers on man his specific character" (p. 275). There is some truth in this statement, but, lacking an analogical and genetic concept of the Absolute, Daim calls idolization (setting up an object as an absolute) what Freud calls fixation (p. 175). Consequently, according to Daim, the fixation of the foetus in the mother's womb is an "idolization." To assert, as he does, that the foetus is and should be in communication with the Absolute is a ludicrous blunder—even on the psychological plane—and explicable only because of the strictly univocal concept of the Absolute which Daim fashions for himself. On the contrary, it would be more enlightening to study this sense of the absolute, on the plane of essences, in its superior analogue and its inferior analogues and, on the plane of existence, in the *via generationis*.

Daim fails to do so and his idea—though interesting for the psychologist, the therapeutist, and the theologian—does not free itself from a permanent confusion. Thus he draws conclusions as dangerous as those of Mrs. Schwartz. He writes for instance:

[194] Charleen Schwartz, "The Confessor and the Analyst," in *Integrity* (April 1956), pp. 12–22.
[195] Wilfried Daim, *Transvaluation de la psychanalyse, l'homme et l'absolu*, Paris, Albin Michel, 1956.

74

Neurosis and, probably, psychosis too, are determined by a constellation which is both functional and religious. In this case, the determining element is the religious factor; however, the drive is supplied by impulses [p. 173].

He even goes so far as to say that "neurosis is, after all, a conflict with God" (p. 145); from which he draws the conclusion: "The day will finally come when everyone who takes himself seriously will submit to a psychoanalysis" (p. 77).

In spite of the sponsors' good intentions and their profession of Catholicism, stands like those taken by Mrs. Schwartz and Dr. Daim —and we could quote others—seem to us as unfaithful to Freudian psychoanalysis as to theology (if not to Catholic theology, at least to Thomistic). They seem dangerous in their therapeutic as well as their pastoral applications.

It would seem that these errors could have been avoided if their authors had possessed the concept of the human act which we have set forth—and, therefore, the concept of a truly moral life. It would seem that this concept—by distinguishing the human act in its essence and its specific qualities from its more or less inferior or analogous participations, but uniting them through integration into one and the same person and seeing them in the progressive stages of their *via generationis*—would enlighten and satisfy the moral theologian as well as the psychoanalyst, be he "humanist" or Christian. It offers one and all some research hypotheses and the possibility of coöperation on theoretical and practical planes, for which so many men of good will are groping.

II.

Pleasure according to
Aristotle, St. Thomas, and Freud

OF all the misdeeds and errors of Kant's ethics, the most serious is probably the discredit he brought upon the place of pleasure in morality and his simplistic rejection of all that seemed to him tainted with eudaemonism.

This Kantian conception seems to us to seriously falsify the laws of human nature, as well as those of divine grace. Besides, it appears to us that a psychological and moral study of pleasure could be a meeting place where the dialogue between Aristotle's disciples and Freud's disciples would have some chance to be possible and fruitful. It is in this perspective that our study is situated.

There is indeed more than one thing in common, especially on the subject of pleasure, between the philosopher-physician of the fourth century before Christ and the physician, tempted by meta-psychology, of the twentieth century. This confrontation of two thoughts—mentalities and intentions—so far apart in time, is all the more interesting for the Catholic moralist or psychologist, in that the "common doctor" of the Church, St. Thomas Aquinas, explicitly takes Aristotle's thought as a basis from which to work out the attitude of moral man towards pleasure.

Before confronting Aristotle and St. Thomas on the one hand and Freud on the other, three remarks seem necessary.

The "Kantian" mentality is older than Kant. Some of its characteristics can be found in the Stoics, through them in certain Fathers of the Church, and later still in the theologians of the end of the

Middle Ages. One can think particularly of William of Ockham[1] whose synthesis influenced so profoundly the moral thought of his successors.

The specific characteristic of this conception is to make obligation or duty the necessary and sufficient, even exclusive, principle of morality, and to refuse it any foundation in nature or in reason. Moral conscience is ruled by an obligation which essentially refers to written law. Thomistic morality, on the contrary, is based on an obligation to do good; it then becomes a question of the obligation of an inner law which orders, from within, the actuation of a nature according to its specificity. The written law is but the pedagogue of the inner law.

The morality of duty and law (the written law) does not allow for pleasure and joy;[2] it reminds one of the "sociological morality" or of the "closed morality" of Bergson. It is the only one that Freud seems to have known.[3]

The second remark is to recall that the Gospel does not present a morality of duty but of love. The entire law (the written law) "depends" on the first two commandments which tell us: "You shall love." The teachings of Christ give the primacy to the "inside," to the animation of the letter by the spirit, to charity.[4] There are indeed commandments, but, in order for them to be practiced truly and fruitfully, they must be animated by charity: "If you love me, you will keep my commandments" (Jn. 14, 15); "Now love means that we live according to his commandments" (2 Jn. 6).

We can thus say, and this is our third remark, that the Catholic tradition—especially until the fourteenth century—gives the primacy to love[5] and joy in its conception of Christian morality. Thus

1 See above, "Introduction," n. 1.

2 See T. A. Wassmer, "Responsibility and Pleasure in Kantian Morality," in *Kant. Studien*, 52 (1960–1961), pp. 452–466.

3 See Pierre Bovet, "Les conditions de l'obligation de conscience," in *Année psychologique* (1912). In the writings of Freud, see particularly *Totem and Taboo*, New York, Norton, 1952, p. 101; "The Interpretation of Dreams," etc.

4 See Th. Deman, "Eudémonisme et charité en théologie morale," in *Ephemerides Theologicae Lovanienses* (1953), pp. 41–57.

5 Ph. Delhaye, "La charité, reine des vertus, heurs et malheurs d'un thème classique," in *Supplément de La Vie Spirituelle*, no. 41 (2e trim. 1957), pp. 135–171.

77

St. Thomas, to the extent that he refers to Aristotle, did not innovate. He merely treated philosophically a traditional theme.

A single testimony from the tradition will suffice to illustrate this affirmation; that of St. Augustine, who so profoundly inspired the whole Middle Ages and St. Thomas in particular.

Hence is it also, if you give good heed, that he says in this place, *No man cometh unto me, save whom the Father shall draw.* Do not imagine that you are drawn against your will: the mind is drawn also by love. Nor ought we to fear, lest by men who weigh words nicely while they are far removed from the understanding of divine things we should, in like manner, be taken to task in respect of this evangelic word of Holy Scripture, and it be said to us, "How can I be said to believe with my good will, if I am drawn?" I say, "You are drawn, not merely by the will, but what is more, by pleasure." What is to be drawn by pleasure? *Delight thyself in the Lord, and he shall give thee the requests of thine heart* (Ps. 37, 4). There is a pleasure of the heart, to which sweet is that bread of heaven. Moreover, if the poet had leave to say: "Each has his dear delight which draws him on" (Virgil, *Eclogues*, 2, 65), not necessity but pleasure; not obligation but delight; how much more strongly ought we to say, that a man is drawn to Christ, when he delights in truth, delights in blessedness, delights in righteousness, delights in everlasting life, all which Christ is? Or while the senses of the body have their pleasures, is the mind left with no pleasure of its own? If the mind has not its pleasures, how is it said, *The sons of men shall trust under the shelter of thy wings: they shall drink deep of the plenteousness of thine House, and of the rushing stream of thy pleasure thou shalt give them to drink: for with thee is the fountain of life, and in thy light shall we see light* (Ps. 36, 8–10)? Give me one that loves, and he feels what I say. Give me one that longs, one that hungers, give me one that is on pilgrimage in this wilderness, who thirsts and pants after the fountain of his eternal home; give me such an one, and he knows what I would say.[6]

"It is true," St. Augustine observes, "that all men will to be blessed, and all will this one thing with the most ardent love, and on account of it will other things whatsoever they may be."[7] This

---

[6] St. Augustine, *Homilies on the Gospel according to St. John and His First Epistle,* London, John Henry Parker 1848, XXVI, p. 4.

[7] St. Augustine, *The Trinity,* in "The Fathers of the Church," series, vol. 45, Washington, D.C., Catholic University Press, 1963, p. 380.

is true "of the evil as of the good."[8] The "good," therefore, are also drawn by the happiness which love gives, and thus by joy.

1. ARISTOTLE AND ST. THOMAS

A. Pleasure

By pleasure we mean any satisfaction of an appetite of man, whether of an intellectual or a sensible nature.

It is, therefore, a question of "the whole family of pleasures," in the words of Aristotle, who writes:

> But the bodily pleasures have appropriated the name of pleasure, which should belong to the whole family of pleasures, because we oftenest steer our course for them and because all men share in them; thus, because they alone are familiar, men think there are no others.[9]

There are thus also pleasures of the intelligence. Aristotle and St. Thomas attribute them to the will, which is for them the capacity of loving beings known by the reasonable intelligence, in short the affectivity of the mind. We must specify that in this vocabulary, pleasure (for St. Thomas: "*delectatio*") is a generic term which covers any satisfaction of an intellectual or sensible appetite. Joy (*gaudium*) is the specific pleasure of intellectual affectivity.[10]

The key to understanding this observation can be found in one of the metaphysical bases of Aristotle's thought which predicates that Being and Good are "convertible"; that is to say, that every being insofar as it is, is good. It is good to exist. Every creature is a potential being; it finds its completion in the actuation of its potentiality; this is therefore its good and that is why it finds therein its joy.

> Whatever is in potentiality, as such, has the desire for its act; and it takes pleasure in its realization, if it be a sentient and cognitive being.[11]

Thus St. Thomas, following Aristotle, thinks that every pleasure is a *quietatio*, a rest, a stop of the movement, a satisfaction of the

---

[8] St. Augustine, *Homilies on the Gospel*, XXVI, p. 4.
[9] Aristotle, *Ethic.*, VII, 13, 1153b 33.
[10] St. Thomas, particularly *Summa Theologica*, Ia IIae 31, 3 and 4.
[11] Ia IIae 27, 3.

desire. This rest must not be considered only as the stop of a moving object which has attained its objective. It is in itself an *affectio*,[12] a *motus animae*,[13] an *operatio*,[14] an activity, says Aristotle.[15] For pleasure is an immanent act, an actuation of the subject who finds in it his perfection.

Pleasure gives to appetite "steadiness and vigor,"[16] because the subject who feels it is enriched by the possession of the object of his love,[17] by the possession of the good loved,[18] because this good "befits" the subject,[19] meeting the needs proper to his nature and to his *habitus* (virtues or vices).[20]

Pleasure also demands possession, that is to say, presence, effective or affective union of the loving subject with the loved object. Without the operation that this union effects, there is no pleasure.[21] In addition, the subject must be aware of this union.[22] This is why beings not endowed with consciousness cannot feel pleasure.[23]

Inasmuch as it is a completion, in act, of the appetite, pleasure has the "realistic" characteristic of love. This is a theme dear to Aristotle and to St. Thomas. For them, the end of the cognitive movement is the subject himself: to know is to draw reality to oneself, to form an image or an idea of it, this representation conforming to the way of being of the cognizing subject: "*Motus cognitivae virtutis terminatur ad animam.*"[24] On the contrary the movement of appetite ends in reality in its extra-subjective existence: "*Motus appetitivae virtutis terminatur ad res:* the movement towards reality belongs intrinsically to appetite."[25]

Let us remark in passing that this realism of love knows, in each

---

[12] Ia IIae 33, 2.   [13] Ia IIae 31, 1.
[14] St. Thomas, *In Ethic. Nic.*, VII, 12.
[15] *Ethic.*, VII, 13, 1153b 7; VII, 12, 1153a 8–10.
[16] St. Thomas, in *IV Sent.*, 49, 3, 1.
[17] "*Delectatio es quaedam quietatio voluntatis in suo volito*" (*S.C.G.*, 1, 90).
[18] Ia IIae 34, 1.   [19] *S.C.G.*, 3, 26.
[20] St. Thomas, *In Ethic. Nic.*, VII. 12; *In IV Sent.*, 49, 3, 2; Ia IIae 32, 2.
[21] *In Ethic. Nic.*, X, 9; Ia IIae 32, 1; 32, 3; 34, 1.
[22] "*Constitui in propriam naturam, cum sentitur, causat delectationem*" (Ia IIae 31, 7).
[23] *In Ethic. Nic.*, X, 8.   [24] St. Thomas, *De Veritate*, 1, 2.
[25] Ia IIae 40, 2.

of us, progressions or regressions. St. Thomas gives us an example of this in his study of the passion of hope, in his answer to the question, classical in his time: "Are youth and drunkenness causes of hope?" To the argument: "The cause of hope is chiefly whatever increases one's power. But youth and drunkenness are united to weakness, therefore they are not causes of hope," St. Thomas replies: "Young people and men in drink are indeed unsteady in reality, but, in their own estimation they are capable, for they know not their shortcomings."[26]

This realistic movement of the appetite is active in pleasure itself, at least in that of intellectual affectivity. The joy felt intensifies the realism of the movement of the appetite: "The lover is not satisfied with a superficial apprehension of the beloved, but strives to gain an intimate knowledge of everything pertaining to the beloved, so as to penetrate in his very soul."[27]

Besides, the loved reality draws to itself the loving subject and tends to mold him to its resemblance (inversely to cognition). The realistic character of love, which makes him who loves go out of himself, is thereby accentuated.[28] Love is "ecstatic," and so is the pleasure which accompanies and perfects it.

St. Thomas, once more quoting Aristotle,[29] makes a distinction which is interesting in that it seems to be close to the Freudian distinction between affects and emotions or feelings.

The distinction is made between two types of desires—and therefore of pleasures—of the appetite of a being endowed with cognition. The first of these pleasures, which Aristotle calls "irrational," is that of the appetite *"ut natura"* or *"appetitus naturalis"*: it does not yet presuppose cognition and is common to any power which attains its own object. The second, which Aristotle calls reasonable, is that of the appetite moved by its object which is presented to it by sensible or intellectual cognition. It is then a question of the desire of concupiscence or of the will as appetite and no longer as nature.[30]

Here are some examples of this distinction.

26 Ia IIae 40, 6.   27 Ia IIae 28, 2.
28 Aristotle, *Rhetorica*, I, 11, 1370a 18; and *Ethic.*, III, 13, 1118b 8–28.
29 St. Thomas, *Compendium Theologiae*, 46.
30 Ia IIae 30, 3.

Hunger and thirst are in the order of natural appetite, whereas gluttony belongs to sensible appetite:

The appetite is twofold. There is the natural appetite, which belongs to the powers of the vegetal soul. In these powers virtue and vice are impossible, since they cannot be subject to reason; wherefore the appetitive power is differentiated from the powers of secretion, digestion, and excretion, and to it hunger and thirst are to be referred. Besides this there is another, the sensitive appetite, and it is in the concupiscence of this appetite that the vice of gluttony consists.[31]

It is thus more exact, St. Thomas observes, to speak of pleasure and pain (*delectatio*) in regard to the natural appetite and rather of joy and sadness in regard to concupiscence.[32]

This distinction leads also to this remark: "Sometimes one feels a certain delight in the body, without rejoicing thereat according to reason."[33]

Here is another example: avarice being more in the order of the "animal" appetite than of the "corporal" appetite, the virtue which regulates the use of money is to be situated among virtues of justice (relationship with others), and not among virtues of temperance (moderation of passions).[34]

One last example will give a better understanding of the distinction we are speaking of: St. Thomas distinguishes the will "*ut natura*" and the will "*ut volontas*." The former necessarily wants the good and happiness, the latter inclines freely towards the objects known by the intelligence.[35]

St. Thomas applies this distinction to love[36] and fear. In this regard he distinguishes the "natural" fear of "corruptive evil" (which nature repels by the natural desire to exist), and the fear of "saddening evil" which is perceived as such and towards which the appetite of concupiscence feels repugnance.[37]

It may be interesting to notice, by the way, that for Aristotle and St. Thomas pleasure is not of itself a "becoming," it is in itself outside of time. It is only insofar as the action which causes pleasure

31 IIa IIae 148, 1; see Ia IIae 30, 3.   32 *In III Sent.*, 27, 1, 2.
33 Ia IIae 31, 3.   34 IIa IIae 117, 5.
35 Ia 41, 2.   36 Ia IIae 63, 1; etc.
37 Ia IIae 41, 3.

is in time that pleasure experiences duration. Of itself, *delectatio* is *"tota simul,"* it culminates in an instant.[38]

The essential question which Aristotle asks himself throughout Books VII and X of *The Nicomachean Ethics* is whether and in what way pleasure is a good, even the sovereign good. He starts from the fact that all, animals and men, seek pleasure.[39]

To seek pleasure is simply to want to act and live:

One might think that all men desire pleasure because they all aim at life; life is an activity, and each man is active about those things and with those faculties that he loves most; e.g., the musician is active with his hearing in reference to tunes, the student with his mind in reference to theoretical questions, and so on in each case; now pleasure completes the activities, and therefore life, which they desire. It is with good reason, then, that they aim at pleasure, too, since for every one it completes life, which is desirable. But whether we choose life for the sake of pleasure or pleasure for the sake of life is a question we may dismiss for the present. For they seem to be bound up together and not to admit of separation, since without activity pleasure does not arise, and every activity is completed by the attendant pleasure.[40]

Let us now ask what is the nature of this perfection which pleasure brings to action.

B. Pleasure, the Perfection of Action

How can this completion which pleasure gives to action be conceived?

First let us read again the passage of Aristotle which has been so often cited on this subject:

Pleasure completes the activity not as the corresponding permanent state does, by its immanence, but as an end which supervenes as the bloom of youth does on those in the prime of their age.[41]

[38] "Pleasures are not processes nor do they all involve process—they are activities and end; nor do they arise when we are acquiring some faculty" (Aristotle, *Ethic.*, VII, 12, 1153b 8–10).

[39] *Ethic.*, VII, 14, 1153b 25.   [40] *Ethic.*, X, 4–5, 1175a 10–20.

[41] *Ibid.* See also on this theme X, 5, 1175b 30, and the expression of St. Thomas: *"Delectatio est quaedam superfloritio naturae"* (*In IV Sent.*, 49, 3, 1).

Therefore, the perfection imparted to action by pleasure is of the order of finality. Which means that pleasure itself is an object of desire.

The whole question comes down to knowing how fittingly to situate this finality of pleasure in a morality based on the attractiveness of Good. What is the end of the moral action: good or pleasure? The pleasure of good, or the good which is pleasure?

St. Thomas, especially in his commentary on *The Nicomachean Ethics,* answers this question "dismissed for the present" by Aristotle as we have just seen.

St. Thomas notices first that pleasure brings to action an extrinsic perfection which is of the order of formal cause. He means by this that pleasure gives it something specific. Indeed, for him, as for Aristotle, action finds its specificity in its object. This is its "intrinsic" specificity which constitutes it in its essence. But pleasure is like a complement of specificity. It is added to the constitutive essence of an action as a consequence of its good functioning.[42] St. Thomas gives the example of sight: the pleasure of seeing which accompanies vision does not constitute its essence. To see is to see, and the pleasure or the sadness which accompanies vision does not modify this one and still less constitutes its essence.[43] It remains that pleasure of seeing can improve the very functioning of sight.

But the order of the perfection which pleasure imparts to action is above all that of final cause. "Pleasure perfects action as an end which supervenes"; to the good which is action comes in addition another good, pleasure, which implicates the rest of appetite in the possessed good.[44] Pleasure being a good, it is normal for it to be desired, that is to say, to act as a final cause.

Is pleasure, then, the ultimate end of man? This would be complete eudaemonism, be it Epicurean or otherwise. This is not Aristotle's position.

In his *Physics* (VIII, 5), Aristotle demonstrates that it is not possible to trace back indefinitely the chain of motive causes. A "first mover," he says, is necessary. Likewise, in human actions, a first mover is necessary. The mover of any act is the end which draws it,

[42] *In Ethic. Nic.,* X, 6. [43] Ia IIae 4, 2.
[44] Ia IIae 33, 4.

84

that towards which it tends. There is really no specifically human life except when man directs himself deliberately towards a "last end," that is to say, towards the accomplishment, the perfection of his being.[45] This end is last if we take the order of execution, but it is first in the order of intention. Other ends are related to it, and they lead to it:

For that which is first in the order of intention, is the principle, as it were, moving the appetite; consequently, if you remove this principle, there will be nothing to move the appetite. On the other hand, the principle in execution is that wherein operation has its beginning; and if this principle be taken away, no one will begin to work. Now the principle in the intention is the last end; while the principle in execution is the first of the things which are ordained to the end.[46]

Our question is, therefore, the following: Is pleasure the last end which a man worthy of the name must give to himself; that which, in the last analysis, he lives for—other "goods" being desirable to him only insofar as they give him pleasure? It is necessary here to distinguish between the sensible appetite and the spiritual appetite. The former has indeed pleasure of its end, but the spiritual appetite does not.

This distinction—which will be very useful when we read what Freud thinks of pleasure—is expressed quite well by St. Thomas, who writes:

The apprehension of the senses does not attain to the universal good, but to some particular good which is delightful. And consequently, according to the sensitive appetite which is in animals, operations are sought for the sake of delight. But the intellect apprehends the universal good, the attainment of which results in delight: wherefore its purpose is directed to good rather than to delight. Hence it is that the Divine intellect, which is the Author of nature, adjusted delights to operations on account of the operations. And we should form our estimate of things not simply according to the order of the sensitive appetite, but rather according to the order of the intellectual.[47]

In animals, sensible pleasure is sought for itself.[48] To the extent that this is true in children, St. Thomas observes, it must not be con-

[45] Ia IIae 89, 6.   [46] Ia IIae 1, 4.
[47] Ia IIae 4, 2; see S.C.G., 3, 26, No. 7.
[48] Ia IIae 4, 2.

cluded that the search for these pleasures is evil, for "they have from God their natural appetite, which is moved to that which is naturally suitable to them."[49] This befits their age and it must be expected that, once adults, they will be capable of "human acts" in order to be able (and to have to) go beyond this "narcissistic" finality of the search of pleasure for itself.

Only the appetite of intelligence has for its specific object the "honest good" and not the good as useful or pleasant. This Aristotelian concept of the *honest good* is capital. Aristotle thereby designates a good which is loved for itself—whatever utility or pleasantness it may otherwise have.[50]

And there are many things we should be keen about even if they brought no pleasure, e.g., seeing, remembering, knowing, possessing the virtues. If pleasures necessarily do accompany these, that makes no odds; we should choose these even if no pleasure resulted.[51]

It is necessary properly to understand the quality of pleasure which this attitude towards the honest good gives. It is generally compared to aesthetic pleasure, in the sense that it is "disinterested," intelligent, and reasonable, open to the universal and the reality of beings, "oblatory."

This pleasure is not sought as the ultimate end. Moral man is not a hedonist. It is precisely because of this that he feels the joy of the accomplished man. It is moral beauty which exerts its attraction on him and which he chooses as his ultimate end. As ultimate end insofar as man hopes for it and approaches it, moral beauty gives him the noblest and the most "human" joy.

If this joy is not his last end, it is not nevertheless forbidden for him to find it good and therefore to desire it. The whole problem is to know which place the "order of reason" and of nature—a nature wounded by original sin—gives to pleasure.

Let us first consider the answer which Aristotle gives to this question. We will see further on the results of original sin and its consequences for the good use of pleasure.

The pleasure of an action is not something extrinsic to it. One and the other are, to take again Aristotle's expression, "bound up

---

49 Ia IIae 34, 1. 50 Ia 5, 6. See *supra,* pp. 40–41.
51 *Ethic.,* X, 3, 1174a 1–7.

together and do not admit of separation." As we have seen, pleasure takes a complementary part in the perfection of action. Therefore, if pleasure is not the last end, it is incorporated into it, it is part of it, it accompanies it normally. "There cannot be a perfect act without delight."[52] The more perfect an act is the more perfect is its delight.[53] "Pleasure is not something extraneous [*extraneum*] to the operation of virtue, but it accompanies it [*concomitans eum*]."[54]

These affirmations of St. Thomas are based on the passage of Aristotle already quoted: "Pleasure completes the activity . . . as an end."

A final observation will allow us to correctly situate the final causality exercised by pleasure. Aristotle and St. Thomas distinguish two kinds of ends, or better, two components of every end: the thing itself, the goodness of which is loved, and the act which permits the attainment of this thing. He gives the example of a miser whose double end is money and the possession of money:[55] "The thing itself which is desired as end, is that which constitutes happiness, and makes man happy; but the attainment of this thing is called happiness."[56]

We can see that these two ends, one of which could be called the objective, the other, the subjective, are but one and that they follow, in relation to each other, a certain dynamic order. It is the object which specifies the act; it gives to the act the term of its intentionality. The act is thereby relative to its object. As for pleasure, it is also part of the end, for it gives to the act its completion; but it is relative to the act which it accompanies.

We can therefore say that an end, and especially the last end, is a reality both complex and one. It includes the thing (object of the appetite), the act which has this thing for object, and the pleasure which is concomitant with this act. These three components are not like three equal parts, more or less connected. They constitute an organic entity, graded, as it were, by an intrinsic finality: pleasure is related to action, which is related to its object.

52 St. Thomas, *In Ethic. Nic.*, X, 6.
53 *In Ethic. Nic.*, X, 9; Ia IIae 32, 8; *In IV Sent.*, 49, 3.
54 Ia IIae 34:3. See *S.C.G.*, 3, 26, no. 8.
55 See Ia IIae 1, 8.   56 Ia IIae 2, 7.

The moral end of man is thus, all in one: the reality of the honest good, the act which gives it to him, and the pleasure which accompanies this act.

It can thus be concluded that the virtuous man's pleasure is included in the last end which he gives to himself. It is included in it, but it is not its only component, not even its main component. The rule of pleasure is in the reality and in the moral honesty of love which is inclined towards this reality. Pleasure is felt in all its truth and its fruitfulness to the extent that it caught up in a movement and in a dynamism which end in and are regulated by Good loved for itself and in its extra-subjective reality.

If this is moral eudaemonism, it seems to us that Aristotle and St. Thomas do not have to be ashamed of it.

C. Pleasure in the Service of Virtue

According to Aristotle, pleasure is not only a formal and final cause of action, virtuous or not, in the secondary and relative way mentioned above; it is also an efficient cause, in the manner of an "indirect agent," St. Thomas states.[57]

Aristotle bases himself on the experience of facts to establish the general principle that pleasure increases the activity which it accompanies:

Each class of things is better judged of and brought to precision by those who engage in the activity with pleasure, e.g., it is those who enjoy geometrical thinking that become geometers and grasp the various propositions better, and, similarly, those who are fond of music or of building, and so on, make progress in their proper function by enjoying it; so the pleasures intensify the activities.[58]

Aristotle continues, noting that

When we enjoy anything very much we do not throw ourselves into anything else, and do one thing only when we are not much pleased by another; e.g., in the theatre the people who eat sweets do so most when the actors are poor.[59]

Further, Aristotle explains why movement is so attractive,[60] and

[57] Ia IIae 33, 4.
[59] *Ibid.*, X, 5, 1175b 7–12.
[58] *Ethic.*, X, 5, 1175a 29.
[60] *Ibid.*, X, 4, 1175a 6–9.

why "the pleasure arising from thinking and learning will make us think and learn all the more."[61]

As St. Thomas, following Aristotle, will say, the fact of taking pleasure in a given activity brings it about that one "is more eagerly intent on it, and carries it out with greater care"[62] and perseverance."[63] On the contrary, "we never do that which we do with sorrow, so well as that which we do with pleasure," for "when we do something that gives pain, the action must of necessity be weakened in consequence."[64]

As good is sought with more promptitude because of the pleasure one finds in it, so evil is avoided more strongly because of the sadness it brings.[65]

One will conclude from this that it is good and desirable to feel pleasure in acting morally well. This pleasure will have a happy effect on the growth of virtues, on the intensity and the quality of morally good acts. "None takes pleasure save in that which is loved in some way,"[66] and this pleasure does nothing but intensify love. To feel joy in doing Good is to increase the love of this Good and the hope for reaching it.[67] Besides, Aristotle observes that the differences between activities are likewise found in the pleasures which accompany them.[68] Pleasures vary therefore in quality. This is especially clear if one compares the pleasures of thought with the pleasures of the senses: "Now the activities of thought differ from those of the senses, and both differ among themselves, in kind; so, therefore, do the pleasures that complete them."[69]

He specifies that "the pleasures of thought are superior in purity to those of the senses,"[70] but that the pleasures of the senses have more "intensity," which explains that many people do not know any other: "The bodily pleasures are pursued because of their violence by those who cannot enjoy other pleasures."[71]

St. Thomas echoes him:

[61] *Ibid.*, VII, 13, 1153a 20–23.
[62] Ia IIae 33, 4.
[63] Ia IIae 4, 1.
[64] Ia IIae 37, 3.
[65] Ia IIae 59, 3.
[66] Ia IIae 27, 4.
[67] Ia IIae 27, 4.
[68] *Ethic.*, X, 5, 1175a 21.
[69] *Ibid.*, X, 5, 1175a 22–28.
[70] *Ibid.*, X, 5, 1175b 36.
[71] *Ibid.*, VII, 15, 1154b 2. See X, 6, 1176b 17–23.

The reason why more seek bodily pleasures is because sensible goods are known better and more generally: and, again, because men need pleasures as remedies for many kinds of sorrow and sadness: and since the majority cannot attain spiritual pleasures, which are proper to the virtuous, hence it is that they turn aside to seek those of the body.[72]

Thus, sensible pleasures can have a "medicinal" effect, a therapeutic effect, we would now say.

In any case, one cannot pretend to do completely without sensible pleasures, "since none can live," St. Thomas says, "without some sensible and bodily pleasure,"[73] and "men need to recreate themselves by some pleasure."[74] To want to be insensible is a vice, for this is to oppose the laws of nature[75] and one can appreciate the remark of Aristotle: "There is also a sort of man who takes *less* delight than he should in bodily things."[76] This is a regrettable disposition and one knows, besides, that the virtue of temperance has for its object to "humanize" sensitivity, and not to kill it.

Moreover, virtue does not rule only pleasure, but also sadness, some excesses of which manifest an absence of authentic virtue. Sadness about things which are in harmony with virtue cannot exist in one who has this virtue, because virtue rejoices in that which is proper to it. But this virtue sorrows moderately for all that for which, in some way, it feels repugnance.[77]

It is, therefore, a natural and immoral misfortune not to know some pleasure in sensible as well as intellectual activities. Not to be able to feel pleasure in the latter places one in danger of turning with intemperance to sensible pleasures. Or else, if one had begun some virtuous action without feeling some pleasure in doing so, there would be much danger for him not to persevere:

No one can long endure anything which saddens him; this is true even of the honest good, if it appears unpleasant to him. Hence it is that men who do not experience pleasure in actions of virtue, cannot persevere therein.[78]

---

[72] Ia IIae 31, 5. [73] Ia IIae 34, 1.
[74] St. Thomas, *In Ethic. Nic.*, VII, 14.
[75] IIa IIae 142, 1.
[76] *Ethic.*, VII, 11, 1151b 23. See *Ibid.*, VII, 8, 1150a 34.
[77] Ia IIae 59, 3.
[78] St. Thomas, *In Ethic. Nic.*, VII, 6.

This sadness or annoyance felt for the honest good is well known by the monastic tradition which named it *acedia*.

This sadness is a sort of "fatigue" or "illness" of the strength of appetite[79] and this is why pleasure, of whatever nature it may be, is a remedy for sadness. St. Thomas will say: "Now just as weariness of the body is dispelled by resting the body, so weariness of the soul must needs be remedied by resting the soul: and the soul's rest is pleasure. Consequently, the remedy for weariness of soul must needs consist in the application of some pleasure, by slackening the tension of the reason's study."[80]

There is in Aristotle the prefiguration of what would today be called a psychotherapy by pleasure, which, in spite of medical "*naïvetés*" of his time, is worth noting here, for it reveals Aristotle's conception of pleasure—a conception which St. Thomas makes his own and on which he comments line by line:[81]

For they have nothing else to enjoy and, besides, a neutral state is painful to many people because of their nature. For the animal nature is always in travail, as the students of natural science also testify, saying that sight and hearing are painful; but we have become used to this, as they maintain. Similarly, while, in youth, people are, owing to the growth that is going on, in a situation like that of drunken men, and youth is pleasant, on the other hand people of excitable nature always need relief; for even their body is ever in torture owing to its special composition, and they are always under the influence of violent desire; but pain is driven out both by the contrary pleasure, and by any chance pleasure if it be strong; and for these reasons they become self-indulgent and bad.[82]

Though limited by the medical ideas of his time, St. Thomas here and there makes remarks full of psychological finesse on pleasure and pain, joy and sorrow, and their interplay. We refer the reader who might be curious about them to the "Treatise on Passions" in the *Summa Theologica*,[83] and here we will only cite this remark: "In every pleasure the appetite is viewed as accepting what it possesses

[79] Ia IIae 38, 1.   [80] IIa IIae 168, 2.
[81] *In Ethic. Nic.*, VII, 14.
[82] Aristotle, *Ethic.*, VII, 14, 1154b 5–14. The Latin translation which St. Thomas used did not speak of "excitable nature" but of "melancholia."
[83] Ia IIae 35–39.

[*habet ut acceptans id quod habet*], and in every sorrow, as avoiding it [*se habet ut fugiens*]."[84]

D. Pleasure, Test of Virtue

Virtue is, among other things, a capacity to choose good. This choice supposes an understanding, or better a judgment, in regard to the end wanted and the means which will best lead to it. Now, in order for the end to exercise its final causality, it must be attractive; it must be desired in its reality and in the pleasure which is expected of it. According to what one is, a reality seems desirable or not, as Aristotle often remarks: "the end appears to each man in a form answering to his character."[85] St. Thomas comments on this very often, especially in this passage:

It is proper to a habit to incline a power to act, and this belongs to a habit, insofar as it makes whatever is suitable to it, to seem good, and whatever is unsuitable, to seem evil. For as the taste judges of savors according to its disposition, even so does the human mind judge of things to be done, according to its habitual disposition. Hence the Philosopher says that *such as a man is, so does the end appear to him.*[86]

Because his appetite is rectified, made reasonable, and humanized by virtue, the virtuous man desires correctly the moral good. Hence the favorable part played by pleasure—experienced or hoped for—in the progress of virtue.

This beneficent role is found again in the judicious choice of the means brought into play to reach an end, a choice which is part of the specific activity of the virtue of prudence.[87] This prudential judgment can be held correctly by a man who, without being virtuous, would know the moral science, but the virtuous man judges rightly as if by instinct. He can thus, Aristotle says, be taken as the norm and measure of moral goodness:

The good man judges each class of things rightly, and in each the truth appears to him. For each state of character has its own ideas of the noble and the pleasant, and perhaps the good man differs from

---

[84] Ia IIae 35, 4.   [85] *Ethic.*, III, 7, 1114a 31.
[86] IIa IIae 24, 11.
[87] See Ia IIae 58, 4; 65, 1; IIa IIae 47.

others most by seeing the truth in each class of things, being as it were the norm and measure of them.[88]

This sureness and exactitude of judgment of the virtuous man is well known by St. Thomas.[89] He calls it "knowledge by connaturalness," and he links it closely with love: "Good causes in the appetitive power, a certain inclination, aptitude of connaturalness in respect of good, and this belongs to the passion of *love*."[90]

It is because the virtuous man has as his specific quality this "aptitude to see the truth" and to judge rightly in regard to the good of man and the pleasure which it gives him, that he is the norm and measure of morality and especially of the morality of pleasure:

The same things do not seem sweet to a man in a fever and a healthy man—nor hot to a weak man and one in good condition. The same happens in other cases. But in all such matters that which appears to the good man is thought to be really so. If this is correct, as it seems to be, and virtue and the good man as such are the measure of each thing, those also will be pleasures which appear so to him, and those things pleasant which he enjoys. If the things he finds tiresome seem pleasant to someone, that is nothing surprising; for men may be ruined and spoilt in many ways; but the things are not pleasant, but only pleasant to these people and to people in this condition. Those which are admittedly disgraceful plainly should not be said to be pleasures, except to a perverted taste.[91]

These pleasures of the virtuous man are essentially those which perfect the activities proper to man,[92] that is to say contemplation, in the sense understood by Aristotle.[93]

Pleasure is thus the best criterion of virtue. It is possible, St. Thomas observes,[94] to do an exterior act of virtue without having this virtue: one can be inclined to do so by fear, for example, or by interest, by habit, even by an exceptional demand of the conscience but which does not suffice to create a virtuous *habitus*. All this is

---

[88] *Ethic.*, III, 4, 1113a 29–32.
[89] St. Thomas *In Ethic. Nic.*, X, 7; Ia IIae 95, 2.
[90] Ia IIae 23, 4.
[91] Aristotle, *Ethic.*, X, 5, 1176a 10–23.
[92] *Ibid.*, X, 5, 1176a 24.   [93] *Ibid.*, X, 6–9.
[94] IIa IIae 32, 1.

not the work of genuine virtue, that is to say of that dynamism acquired by exercise which inclines the virtuous man to love the honest good, in a stable and adapted way. The virtuous man only takes pleasure in doing good. This pleasure is therefore a test of virtue: "One cannot get the pleasure of the just man without being just, nor that of the musical man without being musical, and so on."[95]

Aristotle says, moreover, that "the man who does not rejoice in noble actions is not even good."[96]

St. Thomas, for his part, gives account of this principle when he writes:

The repose of the will and of every appetite in the good is pleasure. And therefore man is reckoned to be good or bad chiefly according to the pleasure of the human will; since that man is good and virtuous who takes pleasure in the works of virtue; and that man evil, who takes pleasure in evil works.[97]

The result of all these Aristotelian and Thomistic considerations is that pleasure, far from being foreign to the moral effort, is one of its causes, formal as well as final and efficient, and for this very reason its surest criterion: he who takes pleasure in doing morally good thereby proves that he is authentically virtuous and his right appreciation of this pleasure is the norm and measure of moral goodness.

E. The Morality of Pleasure

Let us come back to pleasure and to the pleasure of the virtuous action. We recall that morality, in Aristotle's conception, is directed by a love, the love of the honest good. This honest good is the specific object of all the virtues which are to be conceived as the Greek word suggests it, as dynamisms which tend toward a "beatifying" end. This end, as we have seen, includes at once the reality reached, the operation which permits one to reach it and the pleasure which results from it.

Morality is thus directed by a search for Good, which includes

95 *Ethic.*, X, 3, 1173b 28–30.   96 *Ibid.*, I, 9, 1099a 17.
97 Ia IIae 34, 4; see Ia IIae 59, 3.

the happiness of the subject. Morality therefore includes in its finality the search for pleasure and joy, the whole problem being to desire them and to experience them in a way both reasonable and conformable to nature, that is to say, in their relativity to good in their reality extrinsic to the subject.

This Aristotelian conception seems, for St. Thomas, to harmonize very well with Christian revelation. It is this conception which—transposed into a perspective of faith—commands the entire second part of the *Summa Theologica* (the part which deals with what we today call morality).

Having come from God, man returns freely to him.[98] This progress is directed by the desire of happiness.[99] Thus morality finds in this desire its principle and its inner dynamism:

Since, therefore, happiness is to be gained by means of certain acts, we must in due sequence consider human acts, in order to know by what acts we may obtain happiness, and by what acts we are prevented from obtaining it.[100]

This happiness, the object of morality, is in fact a realization of the image and resemblance of God which we are:

As God's substance is His act, the highest likeness of man to God is in respect of some operation. Wherefore, happiness or bliss by which man is made most perfectly conformed to God, and which is the end of human life, consists in an operation.[101]

The search for happiness is therefore included in the finality of all virtue, even including temperance (*ex parte finis operantis*):

The need of this life is regarded as a rule insofar as it is an end. Now it must be observed that sometimes the end of the worker differs from the end of the work, thus it is clear that the end of building is a house, whereas sometimes the end of the builder is profit. Accordingly, the end and rule of temperance itself is happiness; while the

---

[98] Ia IIae, Prologue. [99] Ia IIae 1–5.
[100] Ia IIae 6, Prologue.
[101] Ia IIae 55, 2. Compare this passage: "We hope to obtain an end, because we are suitably moved towards that end and approach thereto; and this implies some action. And a man is moved towards, and approaches the happy end by works of virtue" (Ia IIae 69, 1).

end and rule of the thing it makes use of is the need of human life, to which whatever is useful for life is subordinate.[102]

Besides, pleasure is far from being absent from the end of the virtue of temperance, *ex parte finis operis:* "There are," says St. Thomas, commenting on Aristotle, "pleasures proper to the temperate man. He does not flee them, but on the contrary seeks them."[103]

In the light of this principle which animates the whole morality of St. Thomas, one can think that, just as the secondary ends and the means—St. Thomas's untranslatable *"ea quae sunt ad finem"*—are, in their final causality itself, related, explicitly or not, to the last end, so too the secondary pleasures (sensible or spiritual) are related to perfect beatitude.[104] As a result these pleasures are, in this case, a sort of token, or better a foretaste of eternal beatitude; they find in this the best of their attractiveness and favorable influence on the whole moral life. The knowledge and love of the last end, and the exercise of the infinite and divine character of the potentialities of spiritual affectivity, are more intense and explicit, as the quality of pleasure—which in this case is joy—is better.[105]

Thus the search for pleasure—granted that it is correctly ordered as we have shown it—is far from opposing moral life. On the contrary it brings to it an unquestionable dynamism, and at the same time its criterion.

This general principle applies to each action in particular. The moral goodness or evil of any act is measured according to the end which the subject gives it. When the end of an action is in conformity with the reasonable nature of man, this action is morally good.[106] If an action is morally good, the pleasure and the desire for this pleasure are too; they even add to it a great moral value. If the action is evil, the pleasure is evil, too.

In the moral order, there is a good pleasure, whereby the higher or lower appetite rests in that which is in accord with reason; and an evil

---

[102] IIa IIae 141, 6.   [103] *In Ethic. Nic.,* VII, 12, fine.
[104] See Ia IIae 1, 6; Ia IIae 13, 3.
[105] See *In 1 Sent.,* 1, 4, 1; Ia IIae 30, 3–4; etc.
[106] See Ia IIae 18–21.

pleasure, whereby the appetite rests in that which is discordant from reason and the law of God.[107]

F. The Consequences of Original Sin for the Morality of Pleasure

Is not this optimism, we were about to say this health, of St. Thomas in regard to pleasure, an intellectual view and a practical ignorance of the unhappy consequences of original sin?

St. Thomas knows them well. He knows them so well that he is not afraid to say that before original sin the pleasures of man, including those of the flesh, were more intense than in the sons of Adam and Eve.

Here St. Thomas only makes his own the thought of his master, St. Albert the Great (about whose sources one may legitimately wonder). This thought is interesting for it manifests a whole mentality and the position that these two masters of the thirteenth century give to pleasure in the moral life.

One can judge of this by a text indicative of St. Thomas's thought. To the argument: "In carnal intercourse, man becomes like the beasts, because of the vehement delight he finds therein," he replies:

Beasts are without reason. In this way man becomes, as it were, like them in coition, because he cannot moderate concupiscence. In the state of innocence nothing of this kind would have happened that was not regulated by reason, not because delight of sense was less, as some say (rather indeed would sensible delight have been the greatest in proportion to the greater purity of the body), but because the force of concupiscence would not have so inordinately thrown itself into such pleasure, being curbed by reason, whose place it is not to lessen sensual pleasure, but to prevent the force of concupiscence from cleaving to it immoderately.[108]

Thus for St. Albert the Great and for St. Thomas, the consequences of original sin "wounded" pleasure, as well as the human nature, especially in diminishing its intensity. This loss comes from the insufficiency of reason to moderate pleasure, that is to say to humanize it. The whole difficulty of moral effort, especially concern-

[107] Ia IIae 34, 1; see Ia IIae 34, 1.   [108] Ia 98, 2.

ing passions, comes from their resistance to the regulating action of reason.

We inherited from Adam an anarchic nature which hinders the harmonization of man under the integrating power of the mind, "intelligence and love." Passions do not incline of themselves to the love of the honest good, but play a dissident, "animal," and sensual game. They do not, of themselves, enter under the control of reason which alone can make them open up and regulate themselves according to the extra-subjective reality.

The whole moral problem finally reduces itself to attaining to a correct attitude with regard to pleasures, even to sensible pleasures, just as it is proper to dispose oneself with regard to the honest good: pleasure is not the ultimate end, though it is integrated into it, it is related to reality, and to a reality loved for itself, for its moral beauty, and not essentially for the joy or utility which is expected from it.

We will temporarily conclude this positioning of pleasure in moral life by saying, with St. Thomas, that it is not the greatest intensity in pleasure experienced which is of importance to virtue, but the role played in it by the interior appetite,[109] that is to say by the interior freedom, in the use and the very experience of pleasure.

2. PLEASURE ACCORDING TO FREUD

Before taking up the Freudian point of view on pleasure, it is fitting to recall that psychoanalysis deliberately places itself on a level which is not that of moralists. The latter are above all interested in the free act, that is to say the reasonable and voluntary act, that which St. Thomas calls the "human" act, which he equates with the "moral" act.

On the contrary, Freud seems in his writings to want to ignore this level. He places himself on the level of the acts which we proposed to call pre-human or sub-human.[110] The Freudian contribution, situated at this level, is nevertheless very interesting for the

---

[109] "*Ad virtutem non pertinet quantum sensus exterior delectetur sed quantum appetitus interior ad hujusmodi delectationes afficiatur*" (IIa IIae 153, 2).

[110] See *supra,* "The Moral Act," particularly pp. 47ff.

moralist, for pre-human or sub-human acts are more frequent in the behavior of men than properly human acts. Besides, the former prepare the latter and give them their infra-structure. As such, the pedagogue of morality cannot ignore them.

It is not relevant here to present the Freudian theory of pleasure: "This problem of pleasure is," as de Saussure says,[111] "at the center of every analytic conception. It is linked to the play of impulses, and commands the dynamic and economic processes of our psychic life, it is even inscribed in the painful symptoms of neuroses to draw a secondary advantage from them." We will here bring in only some positions taken by Freud in regard to pleasure, and especially those which seem to give a starting point for a dialogue with the readers of Aristotle.

A. The Pleasure Principle

In "economic" terms, pleasure, according to Freud, is linked to the play of the energizing tensions of the psyche. Its process is thus summed up by de Saussure:

The initial excitation perceived as desire, the act which involves an appeasement of tension, the satiety which annuls the initial excitation, and finally the remembrance of pleasure which is a residual investment of a mnemonic trace.[112]

This quantitative aspect does not exhaust, however, the experience called pleasure:

It cannot be questioned [Freud writes in The Economic Problem of Masochism] that there are agreeable tensions and discharges of these which are not so. . . . It is for this reason that we cannot link pleasure and displeasure to the decrease and increase of tension, though this relation is important. It seems that they do not deal with this quantitative character, but with a factor that we must call qualitative. We would be much more advanced in psychology if we would know what is this qualitative factor.[113]

111 De Saussure, "Métapsychologie du plaisir," in Revue française de psychanalyse (novembre-décembre, 1958), p. 649.
112 Ibid., p. 659.   113 Ibid., p. 656.

This qualitative factor varies, not only in time, at each stage of a subject's libidinal evolution, but also according to the nature of the act: "To each satisfaction corresponds a specific act."[114]

This difference in the quality of pleasure is especially noticeable according to the level where it is experienced: in the primary system (the first in the evolution of an individual) or in the secondary system. The primary pleasure is an *affect*, the secondary, a feeling:

All affect is linked to an impulse (even culpability or shame are aggressive impulses against the ego). Their original source is in the primary system. By opposition all feeling belongs to the secondary system. A man who is neither hungry nor thirsty is tempted by a succulent pear and eats it. Even if originally the energy of the ego comes from a deeper source which has come to invest a preconscious mnemonic trace, the act of this man is not linked to the primary system, it belongs as a whole to the secondary system. His pleasure is no longer an affect, it is a feeling. The distinction of the origin of these two emotions cannot always be made in a categorical way given the numerous degrees of passage which exist between them. This is why many psychoanalysts refused to distinguish them.[115]

B. The Reality Principle

The distinction above seems to go in the same direction as the distinction which Aristotle makes between the appetite as nature and the appetite as appetite.[116] But what is still more interesting for the moralist is the very theme of an essay of Freud entitled *Beyond the Pleasure Principle.* This "beyond" is what he calls the "reality principle," the criterion of the advent of the secondary system:

The first example of the pleasure principle being inhibited in this way is a familiar one which occurs with regularity. We know that the pleasure principle is proper to a primary method of working on the part of the mental apparatus, but that, from the point of view of the self-preservation of the organism among difficulties of the external world, it is from the very outset inefficient and even highly dangerous. Under the influence of the ego's instincts of self-preservation, the pleasure principle is replaced by the *reality principle.* This latter principle does not abandon the intention of ultimately obtaining pleasure, but it

114 *Ibid.*, p. 659.   115 *Ibid.*, p. 657.
116 See *supra*, pp. 81–82.

nevertheless demands and carries into effect the postponement of satisfaction, the abandonment of a number of possibilities of gaining satisfaction and the temporary toleration of unpleasure as a step on the long indirect road to pleasure. The pleasure principle long persists, however, as the method of working employed by the sexual instincts, which are so hard to "educate," and, starting out from those instincts, or in the ego itself, it often succeeds in overcoming the reality principle, to the detriment of the organism as a whole.[117]

This reality principle is one of the functions of the ego:[118]

We can best arrive at the characteristics of the actual ego, insofar as it can be distinguished from the id and from the super-ego, by examining its relation to the outermost superficial portion of the mental apparatus, which we describe as the system *Pcpt.-Cs.* [Perceptual-conscious]. This system is turned towards the external world, it is the medium for the perceptions arising thence, and during its functioning the phenomenon of consciousness arises in it. It is the sense-organ of the entire apparatus; moreover it is receptive not only to excitations from outside but also to those arising from the interior of the mind. We need scarcely look for a justification of the view that the ego is that portion of the id which was modified by the proximity and influence of the external world, which is adopted for the reception of stimuli and as a protective shield against stimuli, comparable to the cortical layer by which a small piece of living substance is surrounded. The relation to the external world has become the decisive factor for the ego; it has taken on the task of representing the external world to the id—fortunately for the id, which could not escape destruction if, in its blind efforts for the satisfaction of its instincts, it

117 Freud, *Beyond the Pleasure Principle,* International Psychoanalytical Library, no. 4, pp. 5–6.

118 Among the recent studies of Freud's disciples, one may cite G. Zilboorg, "The Sense of Reality," in *Psychoanalytic Quarterly* (1941), pp. 183–210; P. C. Racamier, "Propos sur la réalité dans la théorie psychanalytique," and S. Nacht, "Deux visages du réel," in *Revue française de Psychanalyse* (nov.-déc. 1962), pp. 675–710 and 711–714. One will find a good *status questionis* in Austin M. Des Lauriers, *The Experience of Reality in Childhood Schizophrenia,* London, Tavistock Publications, 1952. To be noticed are Fairbairn's position: "The libido does not seek pleasure but the object" (see his work, *Psychoanalytic Studies of the Personality,* London, Tavistock Publications, 1953); and the refutation of this position by Michael Balint (*Problems of Human Pleasure and Behaviour,* International Psychoanalytical Library, no. 51, pp. 281–291). See also David Rapaport, "The Structure of Psychoanalytical Theory," in *Psychological Issues,* vol. II, no. 2, New York, International Universities Press, 1960.

disregarded that supreme external power. In accomplishing this function, the ego must observe the external world, must lay down an accurate picture of it in the memory-traces of its perceptions, and by its exercise of the function of "reality-testing" must put aside whatever in this picture of the external world is an addition derived from internal sources of the excitation. The ego controls the approaches to motility under the id's orders; but between a need and an action it has interposed a postponement in the form of the activity of thought, during which it makes use of the mnemonic residues of experience. In that way it has dethroned the pleasure principle which dominates the course of events in the id without any restriction and has replaced it by the reality principle, which promises more security and greater success.[119]

Because it is totally commanded by the pleasure principle, the primary ego of the id is radically "selfish,"[120] as are dreams which "are all absolutely selfish"[121] and the primary impulses of the unconscious.[122] The secondary ego, on the other hand, is "altruistic,"[123] for it is characterized by the domination of the reality principle:

Wishful cathexis carried to the point of hallucination and a complete generation of unpleasure, involving a complete expenditure of defense, may be described as "psychical primary processes." On the other hand, those processes which are only made possible by a good catharsis of the ego and which represent a moderation of the primary processes may be described as "psychical secondary processes." It will be seen that the *sine qua non* of the latter is a correct exploitation of the indications of reality and that this is only possible when there is inhibition on the part of the ego.[124]

The inhibition of the impulses of the id is therefore indispensable. The ego, by exercising it, permits the reality principle to dominate the impulses:

The first wishing seems to have been a hallucinatory cathecting of the memory of satisfaction. Such hallucinations, however, if they were

[119] Freud, *New Introductory Lectures on Psychoanalysis,* Standard Edition, vol. XXII, pp. 75–76.

[120] Freud, *The Interpretation of Dreams,* Standard Edition, vol. IV, p. 267.

[121] *Ibid.,* p. 322.

[122] Freud, *Instincts and their Vicissitudes* Standard Edition, vol. XIV, p. 134.

[123] Freud, *The Interpretation of Dreams,* Standard Edition, vol. IV, p. 270, note 2.

[124] Freud, *The Origins of Psychoanalysis,* New York, Basic Books, 1954, pp. 388–389.

not to be maintained to the point of exhaustion, proved to be inadequate to bring about the cessation of the need or, accordingly, the pleasure attaching to satisfaction.

A second activity—or, as we put it, the activity of a second system—became necessary, which would not allow the mnemonic cathexis to proceed as far as perception and from there to bind the psychical forces; instead, it diverted the excitation arising from the need along a roundabout path which ultimately, by means of voluntary movement, altered the external world in such a way that it became possible to arrive at a real perception of the object of satisfaction.[125]

The real perception of the object permits the ego to "temper" (as Aristotle would say) the primary impulses of the id. "The ego," Freud says, "represents what may be called reason and common sense."[126]

Should the ego, because of this, not concede anything to the pleasure principle? Quite the contrary. According to Freud, the reality principle is but a "modified" form of the pleasure principle:

I described the type of process found in the unconscious (transfer, displacement, condensation), as the "primary" psychical process, in contradistinction to the "secondary" process which is the one obtaining in our normal waking life. Since all instinctual impulses have the unconscious systems as their point of impact, it is hardly an innovation to say that they obey the primary process. Again, it is not difficult to identify the primary psychical process with Breuer's mobile cathexis and the secondary process with changes in his bound or tonic cathexis. If so, it would be the task of the higher strata of the mental apparatus to bind the instinctual excitation reaching the primary process. A failure to effect this binding would provoke a disturbance analogous to a traumatic neurosis; and only after the binding has been accomplished would it be possible for the dominance of the pleasure principle (and of its modification, the reality principle) to proceed unhindered. Till then the other task of the mental apparatus, the task of mastering or binding excitations, would have precedence—not, indeed, in opposition to the pleasure principle, but independently of it and to some extent in disregard of it.[127]

[125] Freud, *The Interpretation of Dreams*, Standard Edition, vol. V, pp. 598–599.

[126] Freud, *The Ego and the Id*, Standard Edition, vol. XIX, p. 25.

[127] Freud, *Beyond the Pleasure Principle*, International Psychoanalytical Library, p. 44.

C. The Primary Ego and the Secondary Ego

In what way is the pleasure principle found again—modified—in the reality principle? Several of Freud's texts reveal his thought.

He observes first that the reality principle is utilitarian: it gives satisfaction to the pleasure principle, by forcing it to wait and to adapt to the real possibilities:

Just as the pleasure-ego can do nothing but wish, work towards gaining pleasure and avoiding "pain," so the reality-ego need do nothing but strive for what is useful and guard itself against damage. Actually, the substitution of the reality-principle for the pleasure-principle denotes no dethronement of the pleasure-principle, but only a safe-guarding of it. A momentary pleasure, uncertain in its results, is given up, but only in order to gain in the new way an assured pleasure coming later.[128]

This renouncement of the immediate but impossible or detrimental pleasure is always at work during psychoanalytic treatment:

Psychoanalytic work is continually confronted with the task of inducing the patient to renounce an immediate and directly attainable yield of pleasure. He is not asked to renounce all pleasure; that could not, perhaps, be expected of any human being, and even religion is obliged to support its demand that earthly pleasure shall be set aside by promising that it will provide instead an incomparably greater amount of superior pleasure in another world. No, the patient is only asked to renounce such satisfactions as will inevitably have detrimental consequences. His privation is only to be temporary; he has only to learn to exchange an immediate yield of pleasure for a better assured, even though a postponed one. Or, in other words, under the doctor's guidance he is asked to make the *advance from the pleasure principle to the reality principle* by which the mature human being is distinguished from the child.[129]

The type of pleasure experienced by the secondary ego of the reality principle has, Freud says, a quality other than that of the pleasure of the primary ego:

[128] Freud, "Formulations Regarding the Two Principles in Mental Functioning," in *Collected Papers*, London, Hogarth Press, 1953, vol. IV, p. 18.
[129] Freud, *Some Character-types Met with in Psychoanalytic Work*, Standard Edition, vol. XIV, p. 311.

Thus the original *reality-ego*, which distinguished outer and inner by means of a sound objective criterion, changes into a purified *pleasure-ego*, which prizes above all else the quality of pleasure.[130]

The primacy thus given to the reality principle over the (primary) pleasure principle is the characteristic of the adult and Freud observed that: "the supremacy of the pleasure-principle can end in actuality only with complete mental detachment from the parents."[131]

The supremacy of the reality principle exercises itself especially, but not without difficulty, in regard to the sexual instincts:

While the ego goes through its transformation from a *pleasure-ego* into a *reality-ego*, the sexual instincts undergo the changes that lead them from their original auto-erotism through various intermediate phases to object-love in the service of procreation.[132]

But this evolution is often delayed and does not reach its term:

These two factors—auto-erotism and latency period—bring about the result that the mental development of the sexual instincts is delayed and remains far longer in the supremacy of the pleasure-principle, from which in many people it is never able to withdraw itself at all.[133]

This delay in evolution plays an essential part in the predisposition to neurosis. This is what Freud himself says:

An essential part of the mental predisposition to neurosis thus lies in the delayed training of the sexual instincts in the observance of reality.[134]

D. *The Pleasure Principle in Dream, Imagery, and Neurosis*

The supremacy of the "primary" pleasure principle remains entire in dream as well as in the waking dream and in imagery.[135] But besides being surpassed by the reality principle, this supremacy can

---

[130] Freud, "Instincts and their Vicissitudes," in *Collected Papers*, vol. IV, p. 78.
[131] Freud, "Formulations Regarding the Two Principles in Mental Functioning," in *op. cit.*, pp. 14–15, n. 3.
[132] Freud, *ibid.*, p. 19.   [133] Freud, *ibid.*, p. 17.
[134] Freud, *ibid.*, p. 18.   [135] Freud, *ibid.*, pp. 16–17.

know failures in its own level. This is due to the "compulsion to repeat which overrides the pleasure principle."[136] This is also what happens in neurosis.[137] The initial external trauma breaks the barrier, the means of defense against excitations which was efficacious till then, and "at the same time, the pleasure principle is for the moment put out of action."[138]

In neurosis the pleasure principle is still active but in a masochistic way; what normally causes displeasure provokes pleasure, and inversely: "There is no doubt that all neurotic unpleasure is of that kind—pleasure that cannot be felt as such."[139]

As a result the cure must tend to give the patient the ability to reverse his attitude towards pleasure and this by appealing to the reality principle:

There is no doubt that the resistance of the unconscious and preconscious ego operates under the sway of the pleasure principle: it seeks to avoid the unpleasure which would be produced by the liberation of the repressed. Our efforts, on the other hand, are directed towards procuring the toleration of that unpleasure by an appeal to the reality principle.[140]

In his emphasis on the reality principle as a factor of progress, maturation, and psychic health, Freud has a conception of pleasure which can be understood and accepted by a disciple of Aristotle. Freud, indeed, does not seem to want to go further than what the Greek philosopher calls the pleasurable or useful good; but in his private life he overstepped this limit beyond which, as a therapeutist, he did not think he had the right to go. It remains that, as he wrote to Putman in 1915, "Analysis makes for unity, but not necessarily for goodness."[141]

[136] Freud, *Beyond the Pleasure Principle,* International Psychoanalytic Library, p. 25.
[137] Pierre Janet already spoke of a "loss" of the "function of reality" as a character of neurosis. See Pierre Janet, *Les Névroses,* Paris, 1909.
[138] Freud, *Beyond the Pleasure Principle,* p. 36.
[139] *Ibid.,* p. 7.   [140] *Ibid.,* p. 21.
[141] In Ernest Jones, *The Life and Work of Sigmund Freud,* abridged and edited by Lionel Trilling and Steven Marcus, New York, Basic Books, 1961, p. 342.

3. CONCLUSION

We will let the reader reflect himself on the importance of this confrontation between the thought of Aristotle and St. Thomas on the one hand, and of Freud and his disciples on the other. We would like, as a conclusion, to wonder about the slight attention paid to pleasure in the treatises of morality, and, what is more serious still, in education. It would seem that the threat—very real indeed—of an evil use of pleasure prevents one from seeing that one can and should make a good use of it.

How many good people, who are victims of a morality of duty, equate the moral life with the suffering of effort! For them, merit is not measured by charity, but by the pain they experience in "fulfilling their duty." The more it costs, the more moral it is. If they experience some joy they become restless with a blunt sense of culpability and a vague threat of punishment. They seem to be allergic to joy; they cannot tolerate it. In the most serious cases it is a question of the sado-masochism of an hyper-trophied super-ego, to use the psychoanalytic vocabulary.[142]

It seems to us that it would be more consonant with natural and supernatural reality and to the great benefit of education and moral life, to bring into play the "*élan*" and health which a good use of pleasure gives.

Let us first observe, following Aristotle and St. Thomas, that pleasure should be an object of study for the moralist:

> The study of pleasure and pain belongs to the province of the political philosopher; for he is the architect of the end, with a view to which we call one thing bad and another good without qualification. Further, it is one of our necessary tasks to consider them; for not only did we lay it down that moral virtue and vice are concerned with pains and pleasures, but most people say that happiness involves pleasure.[143]

And St. Thomas comments that, as the end of the architect, that is to say the edifice to be built, is in a way the rule which com-

---

[142] See G. Zilboorg, "Le sentiment de culpabilité," in *Supplément de La Vie Spirituelle*, 63 (1962), pp. 524–541.
[143] *Ethic.*, VII, 12, 1152b 1–7.

mands his art, so is pleasure the rule and measure of the moral doctrine. The "moral philosopher" must therefore "necessarily" treat pleasure.[144]

Pleasure is part of the object of morality, as far as it follows naturally all moral activity: "The moral virtues are not all about pleasures and sorrows, as being their proper matter; but as being something resulting from their proper acts."[145]

In this conception, indeed, morality includes pleasure in its object and its end. In its object, because virtue consists essentially, as we have seen, in "humanizing" the pleasures and sorrows of life by regulating them according to man's nature and reason. In its end, for this end consists in the perfect and supernatural happiness of beatitude, and "man is perfected by virtue, for those actions whereby he is directed to happiness."[146]

How should the moralist not give his attention to pleasure, since it accompanies by right all action, since the better the action, the better the pleasure, and since, finally, the pleasure one feels at acting morally is the best encouragement to practice virtue and the surest criterion of morality?

St. Thomas even notices that the virtuous man avoids all sorrow: "*Non solum [tristitiae] superabundantiam fugit virtuosus, sed totaliter omnem tristitiam*" – "It is thus good moral [and psychic] health to seek joy and flee sadness."[147]

Pleasure has, as we have seen, the force of an end, and it even participates in the power of attraction of the objective ultimate end. Thence its dynamism, that of love and of all appetite which, if nothing hinders it, goes spontaneously and naturally into action.[148] "*Trahit sua quemque voluptas!*"

Thence it is, too, that the virtuous man knows the harmony and the integration of his pleasures and joys, contrarily to the sinner who, as St. Thomas shows, is torn within himself, for his reason condemns the pleasures of his senses which, in turn, feel repugnance

---

[144] St. Thomas, *In Ethic. Nic.*, VII, 11.

[145] Ia IIae 59, 4, ad 1.   [146] Ia IIae 62, 1.

[147] *In Ethic. Nic.*, VII, 14.

[148] "*Appetitus, si non sit aliquid prohibens, sequitur motus vel operatio*" (*De Veritate*, 24, 2).

to the joys of his mind; in this the sinner loves himself badly and destroys himself.[149]

Pleasure, thus placed in its exact and right position, would give to morality a better health, a greater force and a better interioriza- tion on the plane of motivations, a power of integration and of accomplishment of which a morality of duty is, by right and in fact, incapable.

In short, morality, understood in this way, would have for its end and criterion the good or bad use of pleasures and joys: "Tell me which are your pleasures and I will tell you who you are." Such are your pleasures, and therefore, too, the objects of your love: "*Talis est quique, qualis ejus dilectio est.*"[150]

Aristotle observed:

It is thought, too, that to enjoy the things we ought and to hate the things we ought has the greatest bearing on the excellence of character. For these things extend right through life, with a weight and power of their own in respect both to virtue and to the happy life, since men choose what is pleasant and avoid what is painful.[151]

The rules of the good use of pleasures and joys have been given by Aristotle and St. Thomas—rules which are not without affinities, on another plane, to the Freudian analyses of the human psyche. It is not a question, indeed, of taking pleasure as one's ultimate end, as the intemperate or sensual man does; but it is a question of relat- ing pleasure to its object, to reality itself, which alone is the organ- izing and final term of the movement of the appetite.

The morally perfect attitude towards pleasure consists, in short, in "using it as if not using it," to adopt St. Paul's expression (1 Cor. 7, 31), that is to say with a perfect inner freedom. This thor- oughly satisfying use of pleasure is made very difficult because of original sin. Consequently to attain it we have to labor through the stages of a reëducation which not only consists in moderating our pleasures (the aim of the virtues of temperance), but also in freely renouncing some of them, even though morally good (the aim of

---

[149] *In Ethic. Nic.,* X, 4.
[150] St. Augustine, *Homilies on the Gospel according to St. John,* XI, 14.
[151] *Ethic.,* X, 1, 1172a 21–25. [The translation has been changed from "on virtue of character" to "on the excellence of character."—Tr.]

Christian and monastic asceticism). Indeed, one could not reach detachment towards pleasure without such renunciations.

The religious state is an exercise and a school for attaining to the perfection of charity. For this it is necessary that a man wholly withdraw his affections from worldly things.[152]

This is a central theme in the ascetic and mystic tradition and especially that of St. John of the Cross. We refer the reader to the lessons of this spiritual master, particularly to Book III, Chapter 19, of *The Ascent of Mount Carmel,* and especially to this passage:

The spiritual man, then, must be very careful of the beginnings of joy in temporal things, lest it should grow from little to be great, and increase from one degree to another. . . . However slight his joy may be, let him quench it at once, and not trust that he shall be able to do it later. . . .

If man will not do this for God, and because Christian perfection requires it, yet because of the temporal advantages, besides the spiritual ones, which such conduct brings with it, he should keep his heart perfectly free from all joys of this kind. In this way . . . he acquires the virtue of generosity, one of the chief attributes of God; and which cannot possibly coexist with avarice. Moreover, he attains to liberty of spirit, clearness of judgment, repose, tranquillity, and peaceful confidence in God, together with the true worship and obedience of the will. He has greater joy and comfort in creatures if he detaches himself from them; and he can have no joy in them if he considers them as his own.[153]

Thus "disappropriated" and integrated into the movement of the appetite, pleasure is in its place and exercises there its favorable power. We think that it should be one of the most essential aims of educators to promote this good use of pleasures, as well as a *"consensus"* of good quality to pleasures.[154] In instigating their good effects in the efficacious love of Good, in awakening men to the best desires and joys,[155] which are those of the mind, they would pre-

[152] IIa IIae 186, 3.

[153] St. John of the Cross, *The Ascent of Mount Carmel,* edited by Allison Peers, London, 1928, vol. III, 19, p. 297.

[154] See Ia IIae 15, 4, ad 1.

[155] See *In Ethic. Nic.,* VII, 14. St. Thomas—like Aristotle, in fact—goes so far as to recognize that "corporal pleasures" may be allowed to people who do not perceive the joys of the intelligence, as long as these pleasures

pare them in the best possible way for the discovery of the joy of God and for the gift of his grace.

One knows that St. Thomas considers the joy found in God as the surest criterion on which one can found the moral certainty that one is in the state of sanctifying grace:

Anyone may know he has grace, when he is conscious of delighting in God, and of despising worldly things, and inasmuch as a man is not conscious of any mortal sin. And thus it is written (Apoc. 3, 17): *To him that overcometh I will give the hidden manna . . . which no man knoweth, but he that receiveth it,* because whoever receives it knows, by experiencing a certain sweetness, which he who does not receive it, does not experience.[156]

This is also the thought of St. Augustine:

The aim and object of our solicitude is enjoyment; by care and fore-thought every man endeavors to secure it for himself. He who searches the heart sees our cares; he who carefully searches the loins sees also what enjoyment is the object of our solicitude. And when he finds our solicitude not directed towards the concupiscence of the flesh, or the concupiscence of the eyes, or the pride of life, all of which pass away like a shadow, but raised upwards to the joys of things eternal, which know neither change or decay, then will God, who searches the hearts and loins, direct the just.[157]

Such a pedagogy of pleasure and joy does not seem to be often brought into play. It is, indeed, delicate and demands much discretion. It seems, however, to be inscribed in man's nature—even from the point of view of psychoanalysis. This pedagogy could find a basis in the explicit teaching of St. Thomas and seems to answer the call of God which invites us to beatitude. As it is said in the Psalm: "O taste and see that the Lord is good! Happy is the man who takes refuge in him" (Ps. 34, 8).

---

do no harm. It is necessary that they experience some pleasures, even if they must warm themselves up to it, in imitation of wine lovers who eat salted foods in order to put themselves in a better disposition to drink.

[156] Ia IIae 112, 5.

[157] St. Augustine, *On the Psalms,* London, Newman Press, London, 1961; Psalms 7, 9, p. 86.

Part Two

A Morality of Sexuality

I.

The Virtue of Chastity.
Nature, Components, Stages

ONE frequently hears the sexual morality of the Church being criti-cized, especially in psychiatric circles. By its interdicts in regard to the sins of the flesh, it is said, this morality contributes to making sex a taboo; it cultivates tyrannical super-egos, propagates in this whole sphere a destructive dread, it is, in short, the source of many neuroses.

Such accusations make the Catholic theologian indignant. He is surprised to see men of good faith—who, in other respects, give evidence of scientific honesty—err so grossly. But one must recog-nize that if such a mistake is possible, it is because these psychia-trists observe in their patients serious or mild troubles which they attribute—not without foundation—to morality as it is too often lived and taught by Christian parents and educators. This "morality" wreaks, indeed, psychic and moral havoc. But it is not Christian. The genuine Catholic morality in regard to sexuality is of another nature.

We would like to address in this study both psychiatrists and Christian educators. We would like to show the former that, if they are too often right, alas, in their clinical observations, they are wrong to make the authentic Catholic morality responsible for them. And we would like to invite the latter to correct their teaching, which often betrays the morality of the Church, and especially that of St. Thomas. We will base ourselves, in fact, on the "common Doctor" of the Church, in order to specify the nature of the virtue of chastity, to show its components and to mark the stages of its growth.

Let the reader be at once warned of the disadvantages of a method of exposition which we could not avoid. We had to resign ourselves to proceed by successive stages, even if we seem to break up what in life is but one. On the contrary, all our effort is to show to what extent, without this view of moral and psychological unity, all study of man is seriously incomplete and falsified. The analysis of the virtue of chastity which we present here thus demands to be superseded by a synthetic view. This will probably be possible only at a second reading. We take the liberty to ask this effort from the reader.

1. CHASTITY AS VIRTUE

Many catechisms and treatises on Christian morality limit themselves to the study of the moral conscience of the commandments of the Decalogue; hence it is that they ignore the dynamism of the subject. They are the expression of a juridical mentality which is very legitimate but incomplete, and which must be given its proper place by an authentic theology, the knowledge and wisdom of God. In the light of this theological "spirit," morality is essentially the study of the progression of man towards God. It studies the dynamism and the acts by which man finds his accomplishment and his happiness in this approach towards his God.

Thus the morality of St. Thomas, as it is analyzed in the *Summa*, is by its very design essentially a study of the dynamisms of man. It begins by the study of the last end of man, beatitude, which acts as the animating principle of specifically human acts. Then it dedicates all its effort to the study of virtues (and vices) which are to be conceived as dynamisms; this is in fact the meaning which the Greek and Latin etymologies (*dynamis, virtus*), as well as the ancient philosophers and the Fathers of the Church, give to this word.

In such a conception, morality neither consists in avoiding sin, nor even in doing good, but in doing good well. One can, in fact, do good without having an authentic virtue, by merely following a "good impulse," through fear or interest:

An act of virtue may be taken in two ways: first materially, thus an act of justice is to do what is just; and such an act of virtue can be without the virtue, since many, without having the habit of justice, do what is just, led by the natural light of reason, or through fear, or in the hope of gain. Secondly, we speak of a thing being an act of justice formally, and thus an act of justice is to do what is just, in the same way as a just man, i.e., with readiness and delight, and such an act of virtue cannot be without the virtue.

Accordingly, alms giving can be materially without charity, but to give alms formally, for God's sake, with delight and readiness, and altogether as one ought, is not possible without charity.[1]

What is virtue, then?

Intelligence and love are in us "potentialities," that is to say, seeds, abilities, which, from childhood till adulthood, develop little by little by being exerted. When these potentialities are sufficiently developed and when they enable us to act with stability, readiness, fortitude, ease, adaptation, and joy, they are said to have acquired a *habitus*. Their initial power has developed, and put on muscles, it is ready to act and to act well. Moral virtues are *habitus* of our potentialities to love. Virtues grouped under the name of justice are "muscled" dynamisms which enable us to love (intelligently) beings who are exterior to us; virtues of temperance are the happy *habitus* of our passional desires (concupiscence), and virtues of fortitude those of our passional aggressiveness (irascibility).

As for the virtue of prudence, if it is an *habitus* of the intelligence, it supposes necessarily and intrinsically the dynamism of a rectified love.[2] In this, prudence is a moral virtue.

To be virtuous is to be disposed to love, and to love well, that is to say as it befits a man. Our acts are the fruits of the harmonious interplay of intelligence and love:[3] they are free, not only nor necessarily in the freedom of choice, but more deeply in this freedom which characterizes an act which I am master of and make my own. By such acts I understand and love beings as they are, I

---

[1] IIa IIae 32, 1, ad 1.   [2] IIa IIae 44, 4 and 13, ad 2.

[3] We translate in this way the "reason" and the "will" of St. Thomas in order to be understood by contemporary readers. For St. Thomas, reason is not what rationalism means by this word; it is human intelligence in its specifically human quality. Moreover, the will is not what we are used to understanding by this word because of several centuries of "voluntarism"; it is the power to love persons and objects known by the intelligence.

establish with them objective and oblatory relations which, by relating me to them in the truth of their nature, relate me to the truth of my own nature and enrich me.

The *habitus,* therefore, is quite a different thing than habit. The latter is a mechanism which works automatically. Its acquisition could be, in the beginning, deliberate, but its automatism takes place on a level inferior to the "human acts" originating in the *habitus.* If its utility is certain, habit is nonetheless very often a threat to the freedom of the mind; left by itself it hardens human behavior. A virtuous man does not have the "habit" of good: he discovers good for each action and performs it with a mind unceasingly freer, younger, stronger, and more efficacious. One possesses an *habitus* (*habere, habitus*), one is master of it; the *habitus* is a principle of liberation and of freedom. Habit, on the contrary, left with its own weight, sinks in the slavery of psychological determinism.

This does not mean that there is no habit in the practice of virtues. As Régamey says so well:

While virtue of science is immediately interdependent with the whole life of the mind, the motive habit comes from synergies which are organized in cellular groups. In short the distinction between habits and *habitus* should not be used as much for designating different functions, as for saying if each function is ensured in a more or less intellectual or automatic way. We do not say purely and simply that the art of drawing is an *habitus* and to sharpen a pencil well a habit, but that this art was in the state of perfect *habitus* in Matisse and that it stays in the state of slavish habit in such a pencil pusher, so proud of his exactness. What is important is to tend towards the most perfect integration, to ensure the most lively presence of the freest mind, continually revivifying mechanisms which may impose their blind repetition, maintaining a virtual attention to automatisms in which the correct processes must be consolidated, recognizing the moments when spontaneity must arise.[4]

There is virtue as soon as there is this spontaneity of the mind being exerted within psychological mechanisms, not only in order to use them, but to give them the flexibility of life and the strength of the *habitus.*

[4] P. Régamey, "Notre éveil spirituel et notre cybernétique," in *La Vie Spirituelle* (octobre, 1955), p. 241.

What is this good which allows one to call a virtuous action good? It is good to act, because it is good to exist; but to be fully good, a human action must adequately satisfy all the demands of its nature. To be morally good, our action must be specifically human, that is to say it must bring into play intelligence and will, freedom and control of oneself. Its object, moreover, must befit human nature and be loved as the end of our activity.[5]

If moral fault is not only an error but a sin, it is because the disorder that we introduce by our faults puts disorder into the world and thereby opposes God's wisdom and will, defiguring his work in the eyes of men. This sabotage of the work of God affects its Creator, it is a transgression of the will of him to whom we owe obedience and respect. The divine law has been given to us on the one hand in order to confirm the law of our nature, to reinforce our duty to obey it and help us to know it better; on the other hand, in regard to the new law of the Gospel, in order to enable us to surpass our nature and to participate in the personal life of God. Even more than the old law, the new law is not first of all a written law; it is the law of our supernaturalized nature, a law inscribed first into life, into the mind, it is an inward demand which the written law only specifies and confirms from without. The new law, St. Thomas says, is "the grace of the Holy Spirit in us,"[6] and Christian perfection consists in the love which is called charity.[7] The obligation towards God remains, for this love is a commandment, but a commandment which changes the nature of the obligation: we must obey God as sons and no longer as servants.

Therefore, the name of "virtue" is given to the *habitus* of our potentialities which enable us to love the true good of our life. Virtues make us capable and ready to order ourselves towards the objects of love which complete us harmoniously.

At the same time as they order us to what is outside ourselves, virtues order us within ourselves. Contrary to sin and vice, which by separating us from God disintegrate us, virtue improves the virtuous subject.

The goodness or perfection of our being is measured in reference

[5] Ia IIae 17.   [6] Ia IIae 106, 1.
[7] See "Loi et Amour," *art. cit.*

119

to God. On the plane of essence, since we are created in the image and resemblance of God and since we are recreated and raised to a participation in the divine life, our perfection is measured in reference to our imitation of God in Jesus Christ. On the existential plane, we originate in God as the work originates in its creator, and our perfection consists in returning towards him by our personal and free acts: God is the final aim of our journey.

"Be perfect as your Father in heaven is perfect."[8]

God is pure act, it is thus by acts and by the full actuation of all our capacities that we resemble him, and progress towards him.

God is love, that is why our perfection consists in loving.

God is simple, that is to say without parts, without divisions, he is wholly himself, outside space and time: our perfection consists principally in the acts of our mind which escape time and space and establish the unity of our being.

This is so for all the qualities we attribute to God: they are the transcendental norms of our perfection. If virtue is good and makes us better, it is because it is love, because it makes us capable of acts which complete us, because it relates us perfectly to the natural and divine world which is exterior to us and thus ensures the integration of our being.

It is not virtue which acts, but the person. The person, by his virtuous actions, extends his power to all that he is. The organism of virtues is a whole which grows in all its members at once; virtues are "connected," it is not possible to completely possess one of them without having all the others. For example, the virtues of temperance and fortitude, which put order into the subject, cannot be exerted without an ordering of the relations with others, and this is the object of justice. None of these virtues is possible without a judicious choice and a strong determination of the means to bring into play in order to reach their aim, and this is the part played by the virtue of prudence.

Finally, on the plane of the grace of God, all the virtues are connected in charity which alone gives them a sanctifying value, which animates them from within by ordering us to a new and divine love. The properly Christian structure of our virtues is, therefore, even more than on the natural plane, an organization of our po-

8 Mt. 5, 48.

tentialities of love, love of God in his transcendence and personal life, love of neighbor in the relations of person to person as well as in the relations between the members of this immense "humano-divine" community which is called the Church. All love, as soon as it is satisfied (or merely begins to be so, if but by hope) brings joy. This is why the practice of virtue is a source of happiness. This joy is the criterion of genuine virtue, its effect and its crowning piece.[9] This does not mean that the Thomistic morality is a hedonism, because the ultimate end which it gives to the moral effort is God (who beatifies) and not our beatitude, and the moral attitude which it expects from the virtuous man is not the love of good because it is useful or pleasant, but because it is a good worthy of being loved for itself (*bonum honestum*).

This conception of virtue does not suppress the search for happiness; it merely puts it in its place. St. Thomas distinguishes three components of our beatitude: the good, the act which gives it to us, the happiness which naturally ensues. These three elements cannot be dissociated; but a kind of hierarchy of function and of finality exists among them: happiness is a "concomitant" effect of the act, it is ordered to the act, which is in turn ordered to its object, good. The more love is spiritual, the more it is realistic, ecstatic, and universal: it is towards good that the virtuous man is oriented and not first towards his happiness—and it is in this way that he reaches authentic happiness. "He who loses his life, finds it."[10]

Such are the main characteristics of virtue. Psychologists and psychiatrists must certainly have noticed more than one trait which must have surprised and pleased them by the bridges which they throw up between their science and authentic moral theology.

Let us add one methodological point: to study the virtue of chastity, it is not enough to recall the teachings of St. Thomas as they are found in the "IIa pars," the part which deals more particularly with morality. For St. Thomas, the study of morality extends throughout the *Summa:* the first part, dedicated to God and the creation, gives to morality its term and its model; the third part, dedicated to Christ, to the Church, to the sacraments and the final

[9] See *supra,* pp. 83ff.   [10] Jn. 12, 25.

121

end, gives to Christian morality what is specific to it, its strength and its orientation.

It is a grave sin of omission when the theologian, after the analysis of a virtue, desired by St. Thomas in the *Summa,* does not reconstitute the synthetic unity of the entire moral organism. A medical student begins, indeed, with anatomy and organic chemistry, but these sciences are not sufficient to make a doctor. After having studied a particular virtue, the theologian must replace it in the concrete richness of its practice: connection with the other virtues (especially with charity), imitation of God and Christ, life in the Church, contribution of the sacraments, concrete state of life (in fact, chastity is exercised in marriage or in the state of consecrated virginity).

It was necessary briefly to recall these principles of Christian morality in the conception of St. Thomas to be able to situate what we have to say about the virtue of chastity.

2. The Virtue of Chastity

A. Its Nature

The virtue of chastity is for St. Thomas one of the forms of the cardinal virtue of temperance. The latter has as its "material" object (that is to say, the matter which it is intended to order) the pleasures of eating, drinking, and sex; the former result from the operations whose aim is to conserve the life of the individual, the latter, that of the species (IIa IIae 141, 4).

These pleasures are essentially those of touch (IIa IIae 141, 4)[11] and secondarily all the pleasures which prepare them by stimulating the desire and the satisfaction.[12] In short, it falls to temperance to moderate all the passions of the concupiscible: love, desire, and

[11] Ia IIae 141, 6. For St. Thomas (and Aristotle), the sense of touch is at the root of all the other senses (*In Analyticorum,* 3, 18; Ia 76, 5; *De Veritate,* 22, 5). The sense of touch is the threshold between vegetal and animal species; in man, it is the awakening to the life of the mind which it conditions. *"Qui sunt melioris tactus sunt melioris intellectus"* (Ia 76, 5). Note that, on this point, Freud did not bring anything really new by observing the link of the "libido" with one part of the body. For St. Thomas also, (passional) love and sensible perceptions are linked to the sense of touch.

[12] See IIa IIae 141, 4, ad 1; 6, ad 2; 142, 2, ad 2 and 3; 144, 5.

pleasure, hatred, aversion, and sadness.[13] As a consequence, temperance moderates the exterior acts since they proceed from the passions (IIa IIae 141, 3).

These pleasures being in man the most natural (and therefore the most vehement) but also the most perturbed by original sin,[14] are particularly difficult to order; hence the eminent importance of temperance.

It is good to emphasize here that, for St. Thomas, these pleasures, the objects of temperance in general and of chastity in particular, are not bad in themselves.

One knows that for St. Thomas, pleasure and joy are natural. To experience them is for man by nature a necessity. Pleasures are the effect and the sign of an accomplishment; they give to action its completion[15] and are a kind of echo of divine beatitude.[16] Pleasure is for the soul a rest (IIa IIae 168, 2) and a sort of therapy for the multiplicity of its sufferings and sorrows (Ia IIae 31, 5). No man can long remain in sadness, or deprive himself of all pleasure (IIa IIae 35, 4).

Morally, pleasure is good or bad according as it is the fruit of a good or bad action (Ia IIae 34, 1 and 4) and as it is not sought principally, but secondarily (Ia IIae 4, 2).

Sexual pleasure is not an exception to this rule. If it is great, it is in order to ensure the continuation of the human race.[17] It was greater still, St. Thomas thinks, before the Fall (Ia 98, 2). Since original sin, however (which consists essentially in a sin of pride), these pleasures are particularly difficult to moderate.[18]

We have said that temperance has as its subject the passions of the concupiscible appetite. It is, in fact, on them that it is exerted and in them that it takes root. But nothing hinders the Thomist from extending the sphere of action of temperance to the bio-psychological substructures of these passions. Following Aristotle and St. Al-

13 See Ia IIae 141, 3; 136, 4, ad 2.
14 See Ia IIae 31, 6; 83, 4, ad 3; IIa IIae 141, 4 and 5.
15 See *supra*, pp. 83ff.   16 IIa IIae 55, 2, ad 3; 55, 3.
17 See Ia IIae 31, 6; IIa Suppl., 49, 1, ad 1.
18 Ia 98, 2, ad 3; IIa IIae 153, 2, ad 2.

bert,[19] St. Thomas,[20] in fact, speaks on many occasions of what he calls the "dispositions of the body," favorable or not to virtue. In this connection he frequently mentions the dispositions of the body to temperance (Ia IIae 63, 1) and to chastity.[21]

The door is thus open to the recent discoveries of organic, hormonal and psychiatric medicine and even of depth psychology. Insofar as they constitute the biological and unconscious matter of the passions, Freudian impulses cannot be ignored by moral theology.

Temperance has therefore as its matter the passions of the concupiscible and especially those of touch, including their biological and unconscious substructures. Its task is to "temper" them. *Temperare* means to put order into, to harmonize the parts of a whole. The human order is "reasonable" (IIa IIae 141, 1), that is to say, that it conforms itself at once to the nature of man and to the nature of the beings who are objects of love. This means particularly that the operations, the sources of the pleasure of touch, are directed according to an end (preservation of the body in regard to eating and drinking, continuation of the species in regard to sex); to put a reasonable order into these pleasures, is to order them according to the act which provokes them (Ia IIae 4, 2) and to its aim. It is unreasonable, that is to say false and against nature, to live in order to eat; it is reasonable to eat in order to live.

In this perspective, the pleasures of eating, drinking and sex are morally healthy and good. Little does it matter if this pleasure is vehement, even if it should hinder the use of reason when it breaks forth, as is the case in the orgasm: this good use of pleasure can be reasonable. What is important above all is not the intensity of pleasure, but the way (oblatory or narcissistic) in which the power to love is affected.

[19] See Barbado, "La physionomie, le tempérament et le caractère d'après saint Albert le Grand et la science moderne," in *Revue Thomiste* (1931), pp. 314–351.

[20] See A. Plé, "St. Thomas and the Psychology of Freud," pp. 332–333. 414.

[21] See Ia IIae 51, 1; 75, 1; 48, 2, ad 1; IIa IIae 141, 1, ad 2; 155, 4, ad 2; 156, 1, ad 2; etc.

To him who objects that the carnal act, because of its vehemence, is opposed to the reasonable "mean" of virtue, St. Thomas replies:

The mean of virtue depends not on quantity, but on conformity with right reason: and consequently the exceeding pleasure attaching to a venereal act directed according to reason, is not opposed to the mean of virtue. Moreover, virtue is not concerned with the amount of pleasure experienced by the external sense, as this depends on the disposition of the body; what matters is how much the interior appetite is affected by that pleasure. Nor does it follow that the act in question is contrary to virtue, from the fact that the free act of reason in considering spiritual things is incompatible with the aforesaid pleasure. For it is not contrary to virtue, if the act of reason be sometimes interrupted for something that is done in accordance with reason, else it would be against virtue for a person to set himself to sleep. That venereal concupiscence and pleasure are not subject to the command and moderation of reason, is due to the punishment of the first sin, inasmuch as the reason, for rebelling against God, deserved that its body should rebel against it [IIa IIae 153, 2].

The virtue of temperance, and more especially of chastity, does not have as its object to suppress desires and pleasures of the senses. The man who turns away from all pleasure is not reasonable (IIa IIae 142, 1), for he opposes his nature and, in this, he sins. In this regard, St. Thomas, following Aristotle,[22] speaks of the vice of insensibility.[23]

It is not the role of virtue to moderate passions in depriving them of all activity; passions must participate in the order of reason within the very exercise of their activity (Ia IIae 59, 5).

For the virtue of temperance to exist, it is necessary not only for reason but also for the passion to be exercised freely and strongly.[24] The passion must participate from within itself in the reasonable love.

The passions are, indeed, "animal." As a consequence of the hylomorphic unity of soul and matter, it is of the nature of the passions to be a unique phenomenon in which organic phenomena and phenomena of psychological consciousness unite constitutionally.

---

22 *Ethic.*, II, 9; III, 14.   23 IIa IIae 142, 1; 152, 2, ad 2; etc.
24 Ia IIae 17, 5, ad 1; 56, 4; 65, 3, ad 1; 58, 3, ad 2.

But in man, because of the unity of the person, it is of the nature of passions to call for the moderation of reason.[25] This moderation, when perfect, is nothing else than an internal and dynamic modification of the passions which makes them participate of themselves in the reasonable order of the powers which are superior to them.

There are, St. Thomas says, two ways in which passions are moderated by the superior powers.

According to the first, this moderation is received passively by the inferior powers. The latter suffer a certain violence, which engenders difficulties and sorrows. This way is imperfect.

In the second way, the lower powers participate actively in the moderation coming from the higher powers; this moderation becomes for them as it were a new nature, an intrinsic disposition, a kind of perfection. In this way, the inferior powers order themselves spontaneously to the reasonable good. They then order themselves to it with facility and pleasure, and when this disposition is stable, one can speak of a *habitus,* that is to say, of a virtue.[26]

We will later on draw practical inferences regarding chastity from this brilliant conception of the virtue of temperance. We must beforehand develop this principle and complete it.

The perfect virtue of temperance does not suppose two acts, one of which would be an order of reason and the other the passive obedience of passion. The virtuous *habitus* perfects passion itself, so that it orders itself spontaneously to the reasonable love. The act of virtue is unique, it is the very act of passion.[27]

Adopting a sentence of Aristotle (*The Nicomachean Ethics* III, 11), St. Thomas can thus write: "Perfection of moral virtue does not wholly take away the passions, but regulates them; for the temperate man desires as he ought to desire and what he ought to desire [*temperati enim est concupiscere sicut oportet et quae oportet*]."[28]

This means concretely that the passions of the temperate man, far from being dead, are in full vitality. Though they remain passions,

[25] Ia IIae 53, 1, ad 1; 58, 3; 74, 1, ad 1; *In Ethic. Nic.,* II, 1.
[26] See *In III Sent.* 23, 1, 1; *De Virtutibus in Communi,* 4, 4, ad 15.
[27] Ia IIae 17, 4; IIIa 19, 2.
[28] See Ia 95, 2, ad 3; IIa IIae 141, 6, ad 2.

they are so profoundly integrated to the human person that they are raised to the point that they desire the superior goods, known by the intelligence and loved by the will. They are raised to the love of the "honest good," that is to say, of moral beauty loved for itself, a good which is no longer sensible and particular, but spiritual and universal.[29] Passion surpasses the level of the "pleasure principle," to participate in that of moral beauty (IIa IIae 145, 3). It is by virtue of this that passion itself, being vitally integrated to the person, makes the subject capable, on the plane of his passional life, of the self-determination and self-control which characterize a mind.[30] The passions become thus subjects of "human" acts.

The temperate man realizes the integration of his person and not its mutilation: his passions experience a completely new quality, a properly human quality, which does not have as its necessary effect to extinguish them; they may be even more vehement, as was the case before the Fall for sexual pleasures. An analogy will give us some understanding of this phenomenon. Music has a sensible effect which is experienced even by certain animals, by primitive people and children; but when he listens to a musical masterpiece, the experienced music lover knows an emotion all the greater as he perceives the soul, peaceful or tormented, of the composer. Because there is intellectual communion, the emotion is but greater and higher. Likewise pleasures of the flesh are not necessarily extinguished when they are virtuous: they change in quality while remaining essentially what they are.

Let us observe that this participation of passion in the love of moral beauty must not be considered as a simple displacement of the energy potential of the individual. St. Thomas knows this process, which he calls *redundantia*[31] and which is not without analogy with what Freud calls the "economical factor."[32] It is a question of a completely different process which is situated on the plane of human acts. Passion is not only passively drawn on by the strength of the movement of the spiritual love, it participates of itself in this love and in its qualities: it loves a good for the good itself and not for

29 Ia IIae 4, 2, ad 2; Ia 80, 2.
30 Ia IIae 56, 4; *De Veritate*, 22, 4, ad 1.
31 See *supra*, p. 57.
32 See Freud, *Beyond the Pleasure Principle*.

127

its own satisfaction, its pleasure is ordered to the object of the pleasant operation; this pleasure is oblatory, to use the language of the psychoanalysts.

This conception of the virtue of chastity is alone faithful to the Gospel: "You have heard that it was said, 'you shall not commit adultery.' But I say to you that every one who looks at a woman lustfully has already committed adultery with her in his heart" (Mt. 5, 27–28).

This is an application of the principle of internalization which gives its spirit to the evangelic morality: "You brood of vipers! How can you speak good, when you are evil? For out of the abundance of the heart the mouth speaks. The good man out of his good treasure brings forth good, and the evil man out of his evil treasure brings forth evil" (Mt. 12, 34–35).

"A sound tree cannot bear evil fruit" (Mt. 7, 18). It is thus a question of improving the sap, of purifying the source. To content oneself with positing an external act, even if it is good, is to fall into the sin of the Pharisees: "Woe to you, Scribes and Pharisees, hypocrites! For you cleanse the outside of the cup and of the plate, but inside you are full of extortion and rapacity. You blind Pharisee! First cleanse the inside of the cup and of the plate, that the outside also may be clean" (Mt. 23, 25–26).

Faithful to the Gospel, the Thomistic conception of virtue also holds out a hand to psychology.

To make ourselves understood by contemporary psychologists, we could say that the virtuous man, and especially the temperate man, is an "integrated" and adult man. The intemperate man, on the contrary, is a dissociated being. What is essential in this principle of moral theology is found again not only on the psychological plane, conscious and unconscious, but even on that of the nervous system. In fact, since the work of Hughlings Jackson, it seems established that nervous illnesses are the effect of a dissolution of the functional unity of the nervous system. For Jackson, the ontogenesis and the phylogenesis of the nervous system follow an evolution which he characterizes in this way:

(1) Evolution is a passage from the most to the least organized; that is to say, from the lowest, well organized centres up to the high-

est, least organized centres; putting this otherwise, the progress is from centres comparatively well organized at birth up to those, the highest centres, which are continually organizing through life. (2) Evolution is a passage from the most simple to the most complex; again, from the lowest to the highest centres. There is no inconsistency whatever in speaking of centres being at the same time most complex and least organized. Suppose a centre to consist of but two sensory and two motor elements; if the sensory and motor elements be well joined, so that "currents" flow easily from the sensory into the motor elements, then that centre, although a very simple one, is highly organized. On the other hand, we can conceive a centre consisting of four sensory and four motor elements, in which, however, the junctions between the sensory and motor elements are so imperfect that the nerve-currents meet with much resistance. Here is a centre twice as complex as the one previously spoken of, but of which we may say that it is only half as well organized. (3) Evolution is a passage from the most automatic to the most voluntary.

The triple conclusion come to is that the highest centres, which are the climax of nervous evolution, and which make up the "organ of mind" (or physical basis of consciousness) are the least organized, the most complex and the most voluntary.[33]

Dissolution follows an opposite movement:

Dissolution being the reverse of the process of evolution just spoken of, little need be said about it here. It is a process of undevelopment; it is a "taking to pieces" in the order from the least organized, from the most complex and most voluntary, towards the most organized, most simple, and most automatic. I have used the word "towards," for, if dissolution were up to and inclusive of the most organized, etc., if, in other words, dissolution were total, the result would be death. I say nothing of total dissolution in these lectures. Dissolution being partial, the condition in every case of it is duplex. The symptomatology of nervous diseases is a double condition; there is a negative and there is a positive element in every case. Evolution not being entirely reversed, some level of evolution is left. Hence the statement, "to be reduced to a lower level of evolution." In more detail: loss of the least organized, most complex, and most voluntary, implies the retention of the more organized, the less complex, and the more automatic.

[33] Hughlings Jackson, "Evolution and Dissolution of the Nervous System" (Croonian Lectures delivered at the Royal College of Physicians, March, 1884), in *Selected Writings of John Hughlings Jackson*, edited by James Taylor, New York, 1958, vol. II, p. 46.

This is not a mere truism, or, if it be, it is one that is often neglected. Disease is said to "cause" the symptoms of insanity. I submit that disease only produces negative mental symptoms answering to the dissolution, and that all elaborate positive mental symptoms (illusions, hallucinations, delusions, and extravagant conduct) are the outcome of the activity of nervous elements untouched by any pathological process; that they arise during activity on the lower level of evolution remaining. The principle may be illustrated in another way, without undue recapitulation. Starting this time with health, the assertion is that each person's normal thought and conduct are, or signify, survivals of the fittest states of what we may call the topmost "layer" of his highest centres: the normal highest level of evolution. Now, suppose that from disease the normal highest level of evolution (the topmost layer) is rendered functionless. This is the dissolution, to which answer the negative symptoms of the patient's insanity. I contend that his positive mental symptoms are still the survivals of his fittest states, are survivals on the lower, but *then* highest, level of evolution. The most absurd mentation, and the most extravagant actions in insane people are the survivals of their fittest states. I say "fittest," not "best"; in this connection the evolutionist has nothing to do with good or bad. We need not wonder that an insane man believes in what we call his illusions; they are his perceptions. His illusions, etc., are not caused by disease, but are the outcome of activity of what is left of him (of what disease has spared), of all there then is of him; his illusions, etc., are his mind.[34]

For Freud also, neurosis is a dissociation. This is, among many others,[35] a significant test:

The unconscious, I explained, was the infantile; it was that part of the self which had become separated from it in infancy, which had not shared the later stages of its development, and which had in consequence become *repressed*. It was the derivatives of this repressed unconscious that were responsible for the involuntary thoughts which constituted his illness.[36]

It is an analogous law which regulates the moral unity. Either the inferior powers participate in the reasonable order (which means objectivity, oblativity, universality, spirituality), as is the case for the virtuous man; or the superior powers are totally annihilated by

[34] *Ibid.*, pp. 46–47.   [35] See *supra*, pp. 55ff.
[36] Freud, "The Rat Man," Standard Edition, vol. X, pp. 177–178.

the inferior ones, which is the case for lunatics (Ia IIae 10, 3). In vicious people, the dissolution is but partial or rather, there is inversion: the superior powers are put at the service of the inferior ones and collaborate actively both in their narcissistic and regressive mode, and in their end (Ia IIae 10, 3).

For Freud, as we have just seen, "the unconscious is the infantile." Let us notice, by the way, that this infantilism had already been observed by Aristotle and St. Thomas, for quite different reasons than those of Freud, one of which, the most important, deserves to be pointed out. The child, St. Thomas explains, is not able to know and to love the moral beauty of the reasonable order; that is why his desire does not care for it. It is just the same in the case of the intemperate man who is infantile insofar as his passions remain foreign to the order of reason (IIa IIae 142, 2).

The temperate man, on the contrary, is no longer a child, he is reasonable in his whole person and in all his activities. His faculties are so strongly and profoundly integrated that the inferior ones, without losing anything of their nature, participate in the superior.

B. *The Stages of Chastity and Its Substructures in the Passions*

Two particular passions incline towards the virtue of temperance: one is called by St. Thomas *verecundia* (which is modesty when it is precisely a question of *chastity*), that is to say the shame aroused by vile thoughts and actions (IIa IIae 144). The second passion is the *honestas,* that is to say the (passional) love of moral beauty (IIa IIae 145).

These two passions deserve to be examined. In seeing which position St. Thomas gives to them in the play of the virtue of temperance, we will better understand what constitutes the perfection of this virtue and, besides, we will establish a new point of contact with contemporary psychology.

Verecundia is a passion. It is a fear, the fear felt in the face of a threatening evil to which one fears to yield.[37] The *verecundia* is the

37 Ia IIae 41–44; IIa IIae 144, 1.

fear of dishonorable actions. It is not the perfect virtue of temperance, for, in order to be felt, the *verecundia* supposes a "mediocre" subject: there is in him a certain love for moral good, but he is also not without inclination for evil (IIa IIae 144, 4). Now, as we have said, in the temperate man, desire inclines of itself towards good, and by no means towards evil. That is why *verecundia* can be called a "good passion," it cannot be called a virtue; it is not a *virtue* in the exact and precise sense of the word (IIa IIae 144, 1). It lacks the participation in the rational order and the freedom which specify virtue.

The *verecundia* is only a "disposition" to the virtue of temperance (IIa IIae 144:4); it establishes its foundations, as St. Ambrose says (*De officiis* I; 43); it is an "integral part" of temperance, but it does not take part in its essence. It is a passion which is not yet completely integrated in the order of reason; when this integration is acquired, the *verecundia* is in a certain way absorbed into the virtue of temperance. Proof of this is given by the fact that virtuous and old men do not experience *verecundia,* because they do not feel threatened with committing dishonorable actions; and thus they do not fear them. If they should nonetheless fall, they would experience *verecundia* (IIa IIae 144, 4). Marriage, for its part, has by right the same effect on *verecundia* (*Supplement* to IIIa 42, 3).

For opposite reasons, the vicious man does not experience *verecundia,* for he feels neither shame nor fear of actions of which he would boast rather than be ashamed (IIa IIae 144, 4).

Besides, *verecundia* is generally more strongly felt in regard to the sins of the flesh which are, however, in themselves, less serious than those of the mind (IIa IIae 144, 2). Modesty—which is *verecundia* in regard to sexual pleasures (see IIa IIae 151, 4)—has more particularly as its object, not so much the carnal act itself, as the sights, kisses, and caresses which are called immodest (IIa IIae 151, 4). All these facts certainly indicate that modesty is not a genuine virtue, but merely a passion.

It can no doubt suffice to prevent bad actions, but the passion of concupiscence is not for all that purified. What prevents the shameful action is the fear of a reproach or of dishonor. That is why one is often less ashamed of doing evil in front of strangers than in front of familiar people (IIa IIae 143). That is why, again, one hides when doing evil (IIa IIae 144, 2). Thus modesty alone does not suffice to make us avoid bad actions and when it succeeds in doing so, desire is not for all that rectified. Therefore, modesty is not a virtue.

St. Thomas observes that perfect virtue is found in but few men (Ia IIae 105, 1), and that most men give way to their passions,[38] and we understand that psychiatrists easily confuse modesty with the virtue of temperance and put the blame on the latter for all the insufficiencies and misdeeds of the former. The theologian agrees with them in observing that most men (and mental patients in particular) are far from having the perfect virtue of temperance and that they usually do not go beyond the level of passional and "premoral" fear which is that of modesty.

A second passion, similar to *verecundia,* but in a certain way opposite to it, completes the passional substructures of the virtue of temperance. St. Thomas calls it *honestas,* which we will translate here by the "sense of moral beauty" or the "sense of honor." It is a passion, a sensible love which inclines us to love the "honest good."

St. Thomas so names a good which is excellent and worthy of honor, because of its spiritual beauty. A good is "pleasant" insofar as it satisfies an appetite; it is "useful" insofar as it is used to reach an end; it is "honest" when it is loved for itself. The love inclined to spiritual goods is in the latter category. This does not prevent it from being pleasant and useful, but it is not loved primarily for these motives (IIa IIae 143, 3). The goodness of the moral order is loved like beauty. Virtues qualify us and enable us to love good for itself; they put us in harmony with other beings and within ourselves; they embellish us.

Loved and produced by virtue, moral beauty shines with a particular splendor in the virtue of temperance. Owing to it, in fact, the radiance of the human mind spreads to the depths of animality and makes it, as it were, incapable of mean and dishonorable actions.[39]

Verecundia is a fear of degrading actions; *honestas* is a love of

38 Ia IIae 81, 2, ad 3; IIa IIae 95, 5, ad 2.
39 IIa IIae 141, 8, ad 1; 145, 4.

good actions. But it is a passional love. It is not the virtue of temperance; it only conditions it (IIa IIae 145, 4). *Honestas* is a favorable passional disposition to virtue; it changes into virtue in proportion as the superior powers of the rational order exert their action.

Let us notice again that the moral sense of most men hardly goes beyond this passional level of *honestas;* they love moral good because they are well disposed to do it, from their good nature or good education. If we do not go beyond this "sense of honor," we simply love the honor which falls to us from our good actions. We then remain at the stage of a pre-morality with social reference; we do not attain to genuine virtue.

These two passions, *verecundia* and *honestas,* must not be confused with the virtue of temperance: they prepare it and dispose to it. They are normal, good, and sufficient in the child; they are insufficient in the adult.

C. *The Resistance of the Passions*

The virtue of temperance exists when the passions participate of themselves and from within in the qualities of the spiritual love. The temperate man loves the honest good with a passional love perfectly harmonized with his spiritual love. The orchestra of his faculties plays in the perfect unity of all his means. This conception may appear utopian and it is so, in fact. Such a virtue of temperance hardly exists in the sons of Adam.

We have now to take into account the consequences of original sin which, by separating us from God, dissociated us, within ourselves as well as from the human group.

Through the bond of original justice being broken, which held together all the powers of the soul in a certain order, each power of the soul tends to its own proper movement, and the more impetuously, as it is stronger [Ia IIae 82, 4].

In an article of the *De Veritate* which we would like to cite in its entirety, St. Thomas notices that the corruption of human nature is not, on the earth, radically healed through grace. The latter leaves us condemned to corporal death and thus also to the inevitable character of sin, at least of venial sin.[40]

St. Thomas thinks, in fact, that if man in his original state was capable of a total integration of his inferior powers into the superior, it was not simply due to the play of natural forces but to the action of grace, which the Church calls original justice. Grace which is given to us by Christ purifies us of personal sin, but it does not cure in us the anarchy of original sin. The virtuous Christian is capable of regulating and controlling the violent movements of concupiscence, but he can not hope for a radical recovery. Such a recovery would be a miracle equal to immortality.

The light of faith gives us some understanding of the disorder which we observe in ourselves and of the impossibility in which we all find ourselves of attaining the perfect virtue of temperance.

In fact, sexual passions, for the very reason of their natural intensity, have a great power of anarchy and of destruction of the person. It is because of this anarchic tendency, and not because of their intensity, that the desires of the flesh strongly resist their integration. Let us recall that there is temperance as soon as these pleasures —while remaining passional—participate in the qualities of spiritual love. Though the passions are by nature able to enter into the superior order, they do not give themselves easily to it, they even put up a strong resistance to it because of the consequences of original sin. The subject who tends towards virtue is somewhat like the leader of a democratic government as regards the opposition:[41] the passions do not blindly obey the order of reason, they have a power of opposition. It is not a question of mastering opposition by the sole force of the police, it is a question of convincing it to collaborate in the common good.

[40] "Necessitas peccandi, saltem venialiter, consequitur necessitatem moriendi. Sed in hac vita necessitas moriendi non tollitur. Ergo nec necessitas peccandi venialiter; et sic nec corruptio sensualitatis . . . Sicut ergo naturaliter homo moritur, nec ad immortalitatem reduci potest nisi miraculose; ita naturaliter concupiscibilis tendit in delectatione, et irascibilis in arduum, praeter ordinis rationem. Unde quod ista corruptio removeatur, non potest esse nisi miraculose virtute supernaturali faciente" (De Veritate, 25, 7).

[41] Aristotle, Politics, I, 3; St. Thomas, Ia 81, 3, ad 2; Ia IIae 56, 4, ad 3; 58, 2. St. Thomas takes also the comparison of the control of man over his spouse (De Veritate, 15, 2, ad 9).

The command of reason has to become imperious and clever at the same time. The ideal of the virtue of temperance still remains, which is neither to suppress nor even to assuage the passions of the flesh, but only to obtain from them that they actively orient themselves to the order of reason (IIa IIae 141, 1). But when they are extremely vehement, this may become impossible: it is necessary to calm them first by having recourse to force.

This effort is negative, but unfortunately necessary in order to then allow a positive effort. "It is accidental to temperance," St. Thomas says, "to repel [*repellere*] superabundant passion . . . this virtue is *per se* competent to moderate [*moderari*] the passions" (Ia 95, 3), that is to say to order them to the action and its object, to make them surpass the pleasure principle in order to reach the oblative order of moral beauty.

It thus behooves the virtue of chastity, in order to accomplish its object, to moderate, to "temper" the passions, and even, when they are too vehement and rebellious, to have recourse to force in order to master them. It is necessary to "correct" them as one corrects a child.[42] But the correction, in this case, too, if it has to use force, must be educative. The struggle against the passions should have no other aim than to favor the awakening of these passions to their participation in the reasonable order. The solution is thus to be sought in a sort of contagion of love and not in fear and brutal repression.

The virtue of chastity thus involves—accidentally and in its first steps—an aspect of compulsion, of struggle, of "*refrenatio.*" It is in the same sense that "continence" acts (IIa IIae 155). The latter is a quality of the will (that is to say of spiritual love and not of the passions of the concupiscible). The "continent" man does not yet have the virtue of chastity: his passions are not ordered to and integrated with the reasonable order. But he resists.[43] There are "two men" in him (see Rom. 7, 14–24), he would like to be temperate, he feels repugnance for shameful actions, he disapproves of them and experiences them at the same time. He is continent if he succeeds in preventing them; he is incontinent if he yields.

---

[42] Aristotle, *Ethic.*, III, 12; St. Thomas, IIa IIae 151, 1.
[43] Ia IIae 70, 3; IIa IIae 155, 1, 3, and 4.

Whoever speaks of resistance speaks of duality (IIa IIae 155, 3). Continence thus cannot be in the appetite of the senses, it is in the superior powers of a man who, powerless to moderate passional desires from within, has no other resort than to intervene with the help of his will in order to suppress them or to prevent them from acting. Reason sees aright, it is "right," but sensible desire is subject to its own movement and the will is caught between reason and desire: it is the will which determines the issue of the conflict. The continent man, whatever may be the vehemence of his desires, decides reasonably to turn away from them; the incontinent man, on the contrary, chooses to follow them in spite of the opposition of his reason. Everything thus takes place on the plane of choice, of self-determination; even if reason plays a part in it, the choice is strictly speaking an act of the will. That is why continence is situated in the will (IIa IIae 155, 3), that is to say, once more, in the potentiality for spiritual love.

As a result continence is not a perfect virtue (IIa IIae 115, 1). It is laudable, but it lacks, in order to be a real virtue, success in integrating the entire person through the intrinsic participation of the lower powers in the higher. Christ did not have continence (IIIa 7, 2). In short, continence comes down to a question of firmness of mind (much more than a question of fear; see IIa IIae 155, 2), but it does not put order in the passions. Continence is only a step towards the perfect virtue of chastity.

For its part, incontinence is a weakness of the mind (IIa IIae 156, 1) which makes it docile to the impulsions of the flesh (IIa IIae 156, 2); it is less grave than intemperance. In the intemperate man the order of the reason is completely and habitually reversed: instead of attracting the inferior powers to its level, the mind submits to them, commits itself to them, makes use of its resources in their service to end up with refinements and perversions unknown by the animals. In the incontinent man, the superior powers yield to the most vehement passions, but they recover themselves more rapidly; they are, except in these moments of resignation, habitually well oriented (IIa IIae 156, 3), and the disorder is thus less great. The incontinent man is unhappy, the intemperate man is joyful: "He rejoices in having sinned, because the sinful act has become connatural to him" (IIa IIae 156, 3).

Thus in St. Thomas's perspective, the virtue of chastity is a perfect virtue because it consists in making sexual desires and joys participate in the reasonable order of the love of moral beauty. But it comes up against a great resistance of the passions become anarchic since original sin. It thus has to work with strength and diplomacy. It is helped, in its very first steps, by the voluntary firmness of continence, by modesty, and the sense of honor.

D. The Virtue of Chastity in the Organism of Virtues

The virtue of chastity is not isolated. Being a *habitus* of the person, it is part of a whole: that of all the other virtues of the subject which, through their growth and concrete exercise, progressively realize his unity, his accomplishment, his specifically human perfection. A study of chastity would thus be gravely incomplete if we did not consider it in its concrete exercise and in its correlation with the other virtues and passions.[44]

As we have seen, the virtue of temperance exercises directly its moderation upon all the passions of the concupiscible, love, desire, pleasure, hatred, aversion, sadness (IIa IIae 147, 2).

Temperance moderates indirectly the passions of the irascible (hope, fear, despair, audacity, and anger). For the principle and the accomplishment of the latter is in concupiscence (Ia IIae 25, 1). "He that is not immoderate in desire is moderate in hope, and grieves moderately for the absence of the things he desires" (IIa IIae 141, 3).

The virtue of chastity is thus, directly or indirectly, the moderator of all the passions: by ordering them to the reasonable good, it contributes to integrating them to the subject, in harmonizing them with one another and in relation to the other virtues.

Besides, the virtue of chastity is not without some connection with the other virtues of temperance: abstinence, sobriety, humility, and all the virtues which moderate behavior, actions, and the use of objects (see IIa IIae 155 to 170).

Virtues are "connected." This means that a virtue is perfect only in the subject who possesses all the others. Each virtue calls upon

[44] See A. Motte, "La chasteté consacrée et ses connexions," in *Supplément de La Vie Spirituelle,* no. 54 (3ème trimestre, 1960), pp. 291–306.

the other in order to exercise itself harmoniously. There is no virtue of temperance without fortitude, prudence and justice. As for the virtue of fortitude, we have already seen all the fortitude there is in temperance (IIa IIae 153, 5), and particularly in continence. In order to be perfect, the virtue of temperance must be prudent and just.

There is no act of virtue which does not necessitate the right judgment and the firm decision which are the very acts of prudence (Ia IIae 58, 4). Thus if the desire of the temperate man is rectified, that is to say, if he passionately loves moral good, in order to obtain the satisfaction of this love, he must judge of its adequacy in the circumstances in which he finds himself, choose the means exactly appropriate for reaching his aim, and firmly decide upon their execution. He is capable of that only if he is prudent. Temperance cannot exist without prudence, which is lacking in vicious people. That is why those who do not have the other virtues and are the slaves of the opposite vice, do not have the virtue of temperance. They may well perform acts of temperance from time to time, either through a certain natural disposition (insofar as "imperfect virtues" are natural to man), or through the acquirement of habit: but dispositions and habits without prudence cannot be perfect virtues (IIa IIae 141, 1).

Inversely, there is no virtue of prudence without temperance. For "intemperance is the chief corruptive of prudence."[45] The temperate man alone is profoundly freed from the so frequent blindness of the passions and from the impulsion which they exercise upon the will.[46] Temperance thus makes man capable of intuition and intelligence (*Contra Gentiles*, II, 81). By rectifying the appetite, temperance enables man to exercise a sort of instinctive judgment in regard to its object; this discretion of the heart is called by St. Thomas knowledge of connaturalness:[47] "He who has the *habitus* of chastity judges of such matters by a kind of connaturalness" (IIa IIae 45, 2).

The reciprocal relations of temperance and justice are perhaps

---

[45] *Ethic.*, VI, 5; IIa IIae 153, 5, ad 1.
[46] IIa IIae 148, 6; 180, 2, ad 3; 113, 1.
[47] See Ia IIae 58, 5; 9, 2, ad 4; It is the application of the principle: *"Talis unusquisque est, talis finis videtur ei"* (IIa IIae 24, 11; etc.), *Ethic.*, III, 5; X, 5; etc.

even more important, especially if one takes the virtue of justice in its broadest sense, which makes it the directive virtue of all our actions, of all our relations with others. To be sure, the virtue of temperance has as its effect to moderate the pleasures which affect man himself in his own body;[48] St. Thomas, however, maintains that "temperance, without justice, would not be a virtue" (Ia IIae 65, 5). This can be easily explained. The virtue of chastity has as its effect to order sexual pleasures to their finality which is the continuation of the human species.[49] If sexual pleasures do not of themselves fall into the sphere of justice, they are nonetheless expressed by exterior acts which, for their part, affect the common good. The continuation of the race is, for the human community, "so excellent" a good (IIa IIae 153, 2) that Aristotle says that there is something divine in the human seed.[50] The acts of the flesh thus greatly concern the virtue of "distributive" justice (which refers to the common good); that is why the legislator intervenes in these questions.[51] They concern also the "commutative" justice (which refers to the good of a person in relation to the good of another person), since the sexual act establishes a relation between two persons and possibly a third: the child. Inversely, the disorder of the sin of lust is not measured only in regard to the disorder of the passions, but also in regard to the disorder which it introduces between the persons whose due honor is violated (IIa IIae 154, 1); sin against justice is still greater in the case of adultery (IIa IIae 154, 1).

If marriage has as its primary end the procreation and the education of children, it constitutes an indivisible society of bodies and souls in which each spouse owes to the other total fidelity (IIIa 29, 2) of his "friendship."[52] A certain natural friendship exists between man and woman. It is said that man is a "social animal," and in addition, that it is in his nature to be a "conjugal animal." This

[48] IIa IIae 142, 6; 117, 6; 59, 2, ad 3.
[49] IIa IIae 153, 3; 88, 11, ad 3.
[50] De Malo, 15, 2; "In semine hominis esse quiddam divinum."
[51] IIa IIae 48, 10, ad 3. De Malo, 15, 2, ad 12.
[52] For St. Thomas, there is friendship in the strict sense only when two or three persons love one another on the plane of the "bonum honestum." There is then friendship between virtuous citizens and the members of the family.

natural friendship between man and woman is not only natural as in the animals, in which it is simply ordered to procreation, but it is also domestic (ordered to satisfy all the needs of the family), and when the spouses are virtuous, their friendship is so too (*In Ethic. Nic.*, VIII, 2), that is to say that they love one another with a love which has all the qualities of "honesty." This conjugal friendship is thus situated on every plane: that of pleasure, "*carnalis copula . . . etiam inter bestios suavem societatem facit*" (*S.C.G.*, 3, 123), that of the sharing of material and human goods, that of the souls whose union is "more important than the union of the bodies and precedes it."[53]

There is then between spouses a "*maxima amicitia*" (*S.C.G.*, 3, 123) the importance of which is evident in the exercise of temperance. In fact, sexual desires and pleasures do not affect only the body; their virtuous ordering cannot be exercised without this reference to others. Does not the virtue of chastity consist precisely in ordering pleasure to its operation and object? The intemperate man thinks only of himself; the temperate man thinks of the person loved and of the child desired. The more temperate he is, the more he thinks of the others; the more temperate he is, the more just he is. Thus there is neither virtue of temperance nor virtue of chastity without virtue of justice and the parts of justice called "potential":[54] friendship, submission, gratitude, veracity, liberality, etc. (see IIa IIae 102–119).

Thus chastity and justice give each other mutual support, the former regulating the sexual passions, the latter the sexual acts in their relation to others.

There is a "potential" part of justice which concerns especially the virtue of chastity: it is the virtue of religion. It rules our actions in our relations with God; now God is not absent from the use we

[53] IIa Suppl., 56, 1; 44, 1; 47, 4, ad 1.

[54] A virtue is called potential when it is more or less analogous to a cardinal virtue, without however satisfying all the requirements of its essence. The potential parts of justice which we cite here, have to do with goodness, the good ordering of the acts with regard to the others (just acts), but the debt does not have the same character that it has in the virtue of justice properly so called; it cannot be paid (in the case of the justice due to God and to our parents), it is not strictly demandable (in the case of social virtues).

141

make of sexual pleasure. As we have said, the disorder of our passions is a betrayal of the order willed by God and inscribed in the exigencies of our nature; it is, besides, a transgression of the commandments which he gave us. For this reason, our attitude towards pleasure establishes us in relation with this transcendent Other, who is our Creator. There is no perfect virtue of temperance without respect, obedience, and worship of God; the intemperate man cannot, insofar as he is intemperate, avoid being irreligious.

The virtues of chastity and religion are especially connected in the particular case of virginity. Normally consecrated by a vow made to God, virtuous virginity consists in renouncing all sexual pleasure, not because one feels repugnance for them, but because one sees therein the matter of a sacrifice which one is happy to make for the glory of God, a greater liberation for the service of God, a total gift to the love of divine realities.[55] In order to be virtuous, virginity demands this religious character. It is a "consecration." All abstinence from pleasure is good only if its motive is reasonable. It is reasonable to abstain, but only in the way which is fitting, that is to say, with joy of the mind, and for an end which is fitting, that is to say, for the glory of God and not for our own glory (IIa IIae 146, 1).

Not, once more, that sexual pleasures necessarily oppose the perfect virtue of chastity. The virtuous use of these pleasures is a good, but to abstain from them in order to belong completely to God is a still greater good (IIa IIae 153, 2).

This virginity is a virtue, a love. The virginity which were neither loved nor wanted but only preserved for motives of fear or disgust for sexual pleasures, is therefore not virtuous. "*It is the spirit that gives life, the flesh is of no avail*" (Jn. 6, 63). We could not overemphasize this point, so much do prejudices distort this Christian perspective of virginity. A text of St. Thomas puts the components of virginity quite well into place:

Now venereal pleasures offer three points for consideration. The first is on the part of the body, viz. the violation of the seal of virginity. The second is the link between that which concerns the soul and that which concerns the body, and this is the resolution of the semen, caus-

55 IIa IIae 152, 2 and 3; 154, 10.

142

ing sensible pleasure. The third is entirely on the part of the soul, namely, the purpose of attaining this pleasure. Of these three the first is accidental to the moral act, which as such must be considered in reference to the soul. The second stands in the relation of matter to the moral act, since the sensible passions are the matters of moral acts. But the third stands in the position of form and complement, because the essence of morality is perfected in that which concerns the reason. Since, then, virginity consists in freedom from the aforesaid corruption, it follows that the integrity of the bodily organ is accidental to virginity; while freedom from pleasure in resolution of the semen is related thereto materially; and the purpose of perpetually abstaining from this pleasure is the formal and completive element in virginity" (IIa IIae 152, 1).

This voluntary purpose of abstaining from sexual pleasure is perfectly virtuous only if it is motivated by the virtue of religion; it is habitually expressed by a vow. This is proof that without the virtue of religion, there is no authentic virtue of virginity.

Thus, contenting ourselves with the most outstanding facts, we can say that the virtue of chastity can be perfect only when associated in its acts with the other cardinal virtues, fortitude, prudence, and justice. It is the coördinated play (variable according to each case) of all these virtues which ensures the integration and the maturity of the human person, within himself as well as in his relations with others.

E. Christian Chastity

The necessities of analysis have constrained us to dismiss until the end the properly Christian aspect of temperance and chastity. In fact, the Christian has only one morality and it is Christian. His entire behavior must be animated by his faith.

We have seen that in fact there has never been a man in the state of "pure nature." Adam owed his perfect integration to the effects of the grace of original justice and not to the possibilities of a nature left to its own strength (De Veritate, 25, 7). The grace of baptism, less effective on this point than that given to Adam, is, however, our only hope for attaining a certain integration. Grace, in fact, is not to be conceived as a foreign element "veneered" on our nature; it is on the contrary our most intimate principle of

143

unity. Because it is a gift of God, grace is not only "one" with our nature, it is its principle of unity. Through original sin we are separated from God, and at the same time dissociated within ourselves and dissociated from the exterior world. By grace we are again united to God and thereby unity is established in ourselves and with others. Though it leaves us radically disunited in the very depth of ourselves, the grace of Christ gives virtues—dynamisms—capable of realizing in us a progressive, though never perfect, harmony of all our spiritual and passional powers.

This relative healing is in a way an effect of the "elevating" aspect of grace. Grace, in fact, is essentially a participation in the intimate life of the divine persons, in imitation of Christ and under the influx of his capital grace. This grace which is in us a sort of second nature, makes us capable of "supernatural" actions which give us God himself for object of knowledge and love.

Our actions must be finalized by this divine object; so, too, our passions, including those of sex. In fact, without this "surplus of soul," it is not possible to attain a relatively perfect integration. It is this superior animation that our passions need in order to be harmoniously integrated.

The Christian knows, through his faith, that his body (and that of his neighbor in Christ) is the temple of God:

> The body is not meant for immorality, but for the Lord, and the Lord for the body. And God raised the Lord and will also raise us up by his power. Do you not know that your bodies are members of Christ? Shall I therefore take the members of Christ and make them members of a prostitute? Never! Do you not know that he who joins himself to a prostitute becomes one body with her? For, as it is written, "The two shall become one." But he who is united to the Lord becomes one spirit with him. Shun immorality. Every other sin which a man commits is outside the body; but the immoral man sins against his own body. Do you not know that your body is a temple of the Holy Spirit within you, which you have from God? You are not your own; you were bought with a price. So glorify God in your body.[56]

Christian chastity is enlightened and motivated by these truths of faith; there ensues a new attitude towards sexual passions: the body itself and its functions are at the service of a new and supernatural

---

[56] 1 Cor. 6, 13–20. See 1 Thess. 4, 4.

life, of a life of the spirit under the impulsion of the Spirit of God, in Jesus Christ dead and resurrected. "And those who belong to Christ Jesus have crucified the flesh with its passions and desires. If we live by the Spirit, let us also walk by the Spirit."[57]

It is in this perspective that Christian virginity and the Christian use of marriage can be justified. And this points out the close connection which exists between Christian chastity and the virtue of faith.

Hope intervenes also: "But our community is in heaven; and from it we await a Savior, the Lord Jesus Christ, who will change our lowly body to be like his glorious body."[58]

This hope for the resurrection gives finally its whole sense to virginity which is then lived as an anticipation of future life. "Every athlete exercises self-control in all things. They do it to receive a perishable wreath, but we an imperishable."[59]

We see then the part played by hope—and despair—in the virtue of chastity: "Certain persons refrain from lustful pleasures chiefly through hope of the glory to come, which hope is removed by despair, so that the latter is a cause of lust, as removing an obstacle thereto" (IIa IIae 153, 4).

The Christian use of marriage has thus a new meaning: it is the "sacrament" of the profound and indissoluble union of Christ and the Church (Eph. 5, 32) and St. Paul goes as far as to say: "Husbands, love your wives, as Christ loved the church" (Eph. 5, 25). Companions of eternity, on account of the charity which links them to each other, the perfect Christian spouses find in their fraternal charity so great a bond and such joy that the ordering of their sexual pleasure is facilitated; the union of their bodies is somewhat diminished in importance. It becomes less necessary, they can without too great an effort abstain from it for a time to devote themselves to prayer (1 Cor. 7, 5) or for other motives inspired by faith or the virtue of prudence. "The appointed time has grown very short," the joys of the flesh lose something of their importance, and their temperate use is thus facilitated: "Let those who have wives live as though they had none" (1 Cor. 7, 29).

[57] Gal. 5, 24–25. See Rom. 5, 14.   [58] Phil. 3, 20–21.
[59] 1 Cor. 9, 25.

One also sees all the role of charity in Christian chastity. It is the love of God which gives its perfection to virginity and marriage. It is through loving each other in the light of their faith and hope that Christian spouses love each other not only as husband and wife but as son and daughter of God, and their children likewise. Animated by charity, Christian chastity is capable of ordering the sexual pleasure of the spouses, not only to its end (procreation and education of the children), not even only to the delectable and honest friendship between them, but also to aims as divine as the multiplication of the members of Christ, their profound union, their eternal destiny.

Inversely, the sins of the flesh become in addition, for the Christian, sins against Christ and the fraternal love he owes to each of his brothers.[60]

Thus all the divine "virtues" which grace gives us must be exercised in chastity. The virtue of chastity is Christian and sanctifying insofar as it participates in this supernatural order, in the reasonable order. It is the love of God and neighbor, the "form" of virtues without which the other virtues could not be fully perfect (IIa IIae 23, 7), which gives its final and divine perfection to chastity. With charity and animated by it, faith and hope actively contribute to it, as do the gifts of the Holy Spirit, and especially the gift of fear.

The latter has as its direct effect to place the virtue of temperance under the habitual impulsion of the Holy Spirit (Ia IIae 19), but it has as its secondary effect to facilitate the exercise of temperance. By this gift, the Christian, rendered faithful to the inspirations of the Spirit, is afraid of offending God. Now man needs particularly the fear of God to turn away from that which exercises on him the most violent attraction.[61]

All this theocentric dynamism (theological virtues and gifts) changes the nature of the virtue of chastity by giving it a new and superior end (Ia IIae 68, 4). Christian chastity is *"infused"*; it is a

---

[60] IIa IIae 54, 2, ad 4; Ia IIae 88, 2; IIIa Suppl., 65, 4 and ad 4; *De Malo*, 14, 1 and 2; 15, 2, ad 6.

[61] IIa IIae 141, 1, ad 3. Note that this fear is much more filial than servile; the filial fear is that of love which fears to be separated from him whom it loves. It is not the *"crainte du gendarme,"* but the fear of a father, and of a father full of kindness for his son.

gift of God owing to which chastity is capable of ordering sexual pleasures to the good revealed by faith, desired and expected by hope, loved by charity. This *"infused"* chastity, totally lost after a single mortal sin, is not able to correct or regulate the corporal dispositions (innate or acquired), favorable or not to virtue. That is why, for example, a repentant and absolved drunk is still very weak to resist his inclination. This work in depth which orders passion from within, is the work of "acquired" chastity—acquired by the subject's own efforts—and remains acquired after the loss of "infused" temperance.[62]

It is in this way that the virtue of chastity, by its complex and wonderful richness, is a power of unity and perfection of the subject; it ensures his integration and his maturation, to speak the language of contemporary psychology. Animated by the life of grace, it sanctifies man at the deepest levels of his being.

In such a conception and practice of chastity, one looks in vain for the least foundation for the accusations of psychologists and psychiatrists.

The authentic virtue of chastity is specifically an ability to love. It enables the virtuous man (that is to say the "dynamic" man) to regulate from within the passions of his flesh which are thus assumed by the mind and harmoniously integrated into the human person. This has for its effect to "denarcissize" the joys of the flesh, raised of themselves to the oblativity of the spiritual love which goes from person to person and not from body to body. The virtue of chastity has as its specific effect not to suppress carnal joys but to order them to something other than themselves. It gives the virtuous man, as an end, not the delectation (of the act), but the (delectable) act and its natural and supernatural effect. In short, the virtue of chastity enables a human person to love with his whole being—in the unity of the flesh and spirit—another human person in his soul and body all in one. This virtue is that of happy spouses for whom time only tightens the fecund union; their mutual fidelity is without difficulty because their carnal union, in its very act, has so

[62] Ia IIae 63, 2, ad 2; 65, 3, ad 2; IIa 89, 1, ad 3.

well become the expression of the unity of their souls that their sexuality desires of itself to participate in their beautiful love and its fecundity. Such spouses have the virtue of chastity.

To be chaste is to love, and to love passionately. It is to know a passion which finds its joy and satisfaction only in the noblest and most total love. The virtue of chastity is the love of love, of fully human love in which flesh and spirit are joined. It is, at once and all in one, a virtuous love of oneself (in the integrated totality and the full flowering of the person), an oblative love of the other as a person, a love of the desired child, a love of the family, the city, and humanity. And, for the Christian, it is also the love of God, the creator of these wonders, the love of God who is Love, the love of Christ and the Church (whose unity is the mysterious model of the union of man and woman), the love of our body and that of the others (because they are temples of God and already possess first fruits of the resurrection), the love of neighbor, finally, in the depth of his person and in his divine vocation. When chastity is not such a love, it is not a genuine Christian virtue.

One can see how gravely parents and educators, even if they are Christian, are mistaken when they believe they do good in sowing the fear, even the terror of sex, in children and adolescents; they do not educate them in virtue: they only stir up the passion of fear called by St. Thomas the *pudicitia*. Indeed it is good to educate them also in modesty, but if the latter is not progressively assumed by a love (that of the virtue of chastity), it is powerless to rectify carnal desire from within, it "repressess" it instead of assuming it in a higher love. This method, even if it avoids sins against the flesh in the present, prepares grave faults, struggles without issue, and neuroses for the future. It only dissociates or destroys a love which virtue alone orders, integrates, and raises.

We must say as much, *mutatis mutandis,* of the passion which St. Thomas calls *honestas* and of the (imperfect) virtue of continence. *Pudicitia, honestas,* continence are but stages towards the perfect virtue of chastity. Indeed, stages must not be bypassed; one must rather pass beyond them in order to tend towards the aim which is to love. The educator who does not see this and limits his efforts to arousing fear and the voluntary effort of continence is seriously unfaithful to Catholic morality. One may even presume that he himself does not have the authentic virtue of chastity and that he communicates his own insufficiencies, difficulties, or neuroses to the children and adolescents in his care.

As we have seen, the genuine virtue of chastity presupposes indeed a perfect integration of flesh and spirit which the consequences of original sin make very difficult, even with the help of grace and charity. Few men reach this high level which is that of virtue, and it is a fact that most men only follow their passions. They are then torn between their sexual passion on the one hand, and their passion of fear (*pudicitia*), their passional love of moral beauty (*honestas*), and their will not to yield to the narcissistic and anarchic pleasure of their carnal passions (continence) on the other. But the role of an educator is precisely to awaken each being to the best of himself; he cannot take mediocrity and the failure of what is best in man as his ideal. He must, on the contrary, put everything into action to arouse the authentic virtue of chastity, that is to say to make those for whose education he is responsible go from the regime of passions to that of virtue, from fear to love. It is to the extent that he is so oriented that he teaches genuine Catholic morality—that of the Gospel and of the "common Doctor" of the Church—; and the latter, far from provoking neurotic troubles, fosters in the faithful the integration, maturity, and oblativity without which there is neither psychological nor moral health.

II.

The Education to Chastity.
Spiritual, Psychological, and Practical
Principles of Religious Chastity

1. SPIRITUAL AND PSYCHOLOGICAL PRINCIPLES

A. Modesty and Chastity

To speak and to hear about sexual questions always provokes a certain embarrassment. Instinctively, the speaker obscures his words, and the auditor is uneasy. This embarrassment is of long standing, going back to original sin. "Then the eyes of both were opened, and they knew that they were naked; and they sewed fig leaves together and made themselves aprons. And they heard the sound of the Lord God walking in the garden in the cool of the day, and the man and wife hid themselves from the presence of the Lord God among the trees of the garden" (Gen. 3, 7–9).

Let us not take lightly the meaning of such a primitive gesture, the need to cover, to veil, to hide oneself, to flee as soon as it is a question of sexuality. This attitude, so characteristic, is at the heart of our subject.

Here are some examples. It is significant that the very word "chastity" cannot pass through certain pious lips, which speak more willingly of the "holy virtue," as if to speak of chastity were already to fail in it.

More serious and more symptomatic is the following fact: during the numerous tests for the discrimination of vocations which we

150

conduct, we always take care to inform ourselves about the way the candidate, when he was a child or an adolescent, was informed about the sexual realities. Most often, the parents preserve a complete silence or, at the best, give a few explanations, almost always awkward. And even we confessors and educators, are not we embarrassed when we have to deal with these questions? And yet the absence of an answer to a legitimate curiosity, and the terrible solitude in which the great majority of adolescents struggle, very often prevent this crisis of growth from being resolved as it should be.

We must observe, besides, that most scandals are fed by sexual faults more often imagined and spread than really perpetuated and verified, especially when consecrated persons are compromised in them. It is a great delight for a person as prudish as easily scandalized, to have the opportunity of giving himself the double joy of stirring up as much mud as possible, on the one hand, and of feeling the comforting satisfaction of a good conscience on the other, for if he allows himself to speak of these "things" it is in order to condemn them all the more vehemently as the temptation to succumb to them is stronger! "He who loves his brother abides in the light, and in it there is no cause for stumbling" (1 Jn. 2, 10), and we take the liberty of adding: he who is truly and profoundly chaste is not easily scandalized.

The attitude of our Lord, each time he is confronted with a fault of the flesh, is full of lessons: "Go, and do not sin again" (Jn. 8, 11), "Therefore I tell you, her sins, which are many, are forgiven, for she loved much" (Lk. 7, 47); this attitude is in violent contrast with his anger and maledictions again the Parisees. Besides the Lord knows very well the secret culpability which embarrasses every one of us: "Let him who is without sin among you be the first to throw a stone at her" (Jn. 8, 7).

It is then a well established fact that there is a sort of general and personal culpability around these questions. It is an emotional guilt, or rather in the words of St. Thomas, a passional guilt,[1] which he is very careful to distinguish from genuine culpability, that is to say, contrition. To say it right away, it seems to us that this passional culpability, conscious or unconscious, does generally more evil than

[1] See IIIa Suppl., 1, 2, ad 1.

good, especially when it becomes obsessional, as in people who masturbate.

As we were saying in the beginning, this embarrassment, this need of veiling oneself is accompanied by the desire to hide oneself from the threatening look of the moral authority. This is as old as the first sin: "But the Lord God called to the man, and said to him, 'Where are you?' And he said, 'I heard the sound of thee in the garden, and I was afraid, because I was naked; and I hid myself' " (Gen. 3, 9–10).

What is then the meaning of this fear? This sort of shame bears a name in the Christian tradition; it is *"verecundia,"* which corresponds approximately to what we understand by "modesty."

In his great wisdom, St. Thomas asserts and shows why modesty is not a virtue in the proper sense of the word (IIa IIae 144). It is a passion, a passional fear whose movement is not reasonable and free, but proceeds *"ex impetu quodam passionis"* (IIa IIae 144, 1). It is indeed a laudable passion, but, as we will reiterate below, modesty is not the virtue of chastity: it is not a spiritual and free love of chastity, it is only the fear of moral punishment, especially in its social reference.

Shamefacedness regards fault in two ways. In one way a man refrains from vicious acts through fear of reproach: in another way a man while doing a disgraceful deed avoids the public eye through fear of reproach [IIa IIae 144, 2].

Modesty is so slightly, by itself, an authentic virtue, that for St. Thomas genuinely virtuous people hardly experience it. This is exactly how he expresses himself:

Shame may be lacking in a person in two ways. First, because the things that should make him ashamed are not deemed by him to be disgraceful; and in this way those who are steeped in sin are without shame, for instead of disapproving of their sins, they boast of them. Secondly, because they apprehend disgrace as impossible to themselves, or as easy to avoid. In this way the old and the virtuous are not shamefaced. Yet they are so disposed, that if there were anything disgraceful in them they would be ashamed of it [IIa IIae 144, 4].

152

We wanted to speak of modesty in the beginning, first in order to place us if possible, you and me, in the attitude of old and virtuous people, and to thus allow us to speak of our chastity with the serenity and objectivity of virtue, and not with the embarrassment and veils of modesty; secondly, because the psycho-physiological science which is called sexology hardly raises itself beyond the passional world of modesty. This constitutes at once its richness —for on this level it can bring us a great deal—, and its radical insufficiency: all too often it ignores the genuine virtue of chastity.

B. *The Richness and Limits of Sexology*

It is not the place here to write a treatise on sexology. We would only like to mention some of its principles, relatively new, which can throw some light on our reflexions.

The first of these contributions is based on animal psychology. Observations and experiments have in fact shown that, even in animals, physiology and hormonal secretions are far from being sufficient to explain their sexual behavior. The very important role played by "sign-stimuli," which are a psycho-social phenomenon, has been observed. This is, for example, what Paul Fraisse, director of the Institute of Psychology at the Sorbonne, says:

Everyone knows the case of the pigeon in which sexual maturity does not occur if it is raised alone. In a more general way there are what Grassé calls group effects. On the part of the members of the species each individual is subject to an interplay of optical, acoustical, olfactory stimulations which, acting upon the neuro-endocrine regulations, provoke additional secretions. It has thus been observed in colonies of sea-gulls that the more numerous they are, the sooner the egg-laying season occurs. It has indeed been possible to show clearly the effects peculiar to imitation. Thus, if male hormone is injected into some birds (the colins of California) living in colony, two months before the breeding season, one can observe that two days later these birds try to copulate, which is but a biological effect. But ten days later the birds of the colony which did not undergo the treatment begin also to pair off: the example produced an excitatory effect. This fact can be observed also, though in a less spectacular way, in numerous species in which display and copulation of some individuals provoke the same behavior in others hitherto passive.[2]

If this is true of animals, how much more so of man! The sexual instinct has indeed a physiological and endocrinological basis, but the psychological and sociological factors play an extensive role. From this point of view we make our own the affirmation of the director of the neuro-physiological laboratory of the Ecole des Hautes Etudes at the Sorbonne, Paul Chauchard: "The principal sexual organ of man is the brain."[3]

This orientation of the studies in sexology is complemented with a second which could be formulated this way: the fact of being sexed is neither limited to the anatomical and functional difference of the genitals, nor even to what is called the secondary sexual characteristics, but to the entire being, and on all levels. Man and woman have indeed the same nature, but their way of being human is different, from their structural and evolutional physiology to their psychology and the type of their relations with other human beings. These differences are already inscribed in the chromosomes of the mother-cell, and develop little by little, depending not only on physiological growth, but also on the cultural environment and on all the socio-psycho-physiological determinations of each individual. This extension of sexuality to our whole being and all that it implies opens a very wide field to the domain of the virtue of chastity and to its pedagogy.

Another direction in which sexology is progressing is this: the normal sexual life of the adult is not an eroticism; on the contrary it is the expression (and the education) of and harmonic fusion of sexuality and affection. Oswald Schwartz writes in his book *Psychologie sexuelle:* "It is only in a human being who has reached his perfection, his full maturity, that we find the indefectible fusion of love and the sexual impulse."[4]

[2] See Paul Fraisse, "Les deux sources de la sexualité," in *Esprit* (novembre, 1960), p. 1727. For further details see the work of Louis Bounoure, *L'instinct sexuel, étude de psychologie animale,* P.U.F., 1956, particularly about the pigeons, p. 33, and the colins of California, p. 34.

[3] Paul Chauchard, *La maîtrise sexuelle,* Paris, Editions du Levain, 1962, p. 20.

[4] *Psychologie sexuelle,* P.U.F., 1952, p. 7.

154

This means—and it is still another direction of the work in sexology—that sexual activity is a privileged mode, and in a certain way the richest mode, of relation to others, of the way of being in the world, as the existentialists say. The normal and completed sexual act is communication, reciprocal gift between two persons. It is a language of the body, or rather a language of the soul through the body—a language, a dialogue of the whole being. The relation to the partner is part of the very essence and the end of sexual life. Thus sexual activity—or the abstention from it—has a very general signification which surpasses by far simple genitality. We will refer to a novelist, Graham Greene, to illustrate this affirmation:

"Can you explain away love too?" I asked.

"Oh, yes," he said. "The desire to possess in some, like avarice; in others the desire to surrender, to lose the sense of responsibility, the wish to be admired. Sometimes just the wish to be able to talk, to unburden yourself to someone who won't be bored. The desire to find again a father or a mother. And of course under it all the biological motive."

I thought, it's all true, but isn't there something over? I've dug up all that in myself, in Maurice too, but still the spade hasn't touched rock. "And the love of God?" I asked him.[5]

It will be easy for us to draw from all these principles useful consequences for our study. We have still, beforehand, to enumerate some principles of a psychology which has a very bad reputation, at least with those who know it only by hearsay, or who have a second-hand knowledge of it. We mean Freudian psychology.

We hope not to shock anybody in asserting here that in our eyes it is to lack intellectual honesty to repeat the condemnation, very widespread, alas, according to which Freud would be pansexualist. It is true that some disciples of Freud are so, but the master whom they claim is not, nor are the majority of his most serious disciples. We will give only one proof of this by quoting a passage of the *Introductory Lectures on Psychoanalysis:*

On the other hand, the abandonment of the reproductive function is the common feature of all perversions. We actually describe a sexual activity as perverse if it has given up the aim of reproduction and

[5] *The End of the Affair,* New York, Viking Press, 1961, p. 130.

155

pursues the attainment of pleasure as an aim independent of it. So, as you will see, the breach and turning-point in the development of sexual life lies in its becoming subordinate to the purposes of reproduction. Everything that happens before this turn of events and equally everything that disregards it and that aims solely at obtaining pleasure is given the uncomplimentary name of "perverse" and as such is proscribed.[6]

Certain Freudian positions of interest to our subject are not without points of contact in their way with the Aristotelian-Thomistic theses.[7]

Freud distinguishes two fundamental and in some way antagonistic impulses: the libido and aggressiveness. This distinction has the same general orientation as that, dear to Aristotle and St. Thomas, of our sensible appetites, concupiscible and irascible.

The Freudian libido is attached to erogenous zones of the body. Freud says, for example:

We next found that sexual excitation in children springs from a multiplicity of forces. Satisfaction arises first and foremost from the appropriate sensory excitation of what we have described as erotogenic zones. It seems probable that any part of the skin and any sense-organ— probably, indeed, *any* organ—can function as an erotogenic zone, though there are some particularly marked erotogenic zones whose excitation would seem to be secured from the very first by certain organic contrivances.[8]

Let us recall regarding this point that for St. Thomas, the (material) object of the virtue of temperance are the pleasures of touch. *"Temperentia est circa delectatione tactus"* (IIa IIae 141, 4). Now, if we are willing to understand honestly the vocabulary of Freud who calls genital what we usually call sexual, and sexual any pleasure linked to touch, we are not scandalized but enlightened by the analysis which he gives of "sexual" pleasure, even in the child.

We are also indebted to Freud for having reintroduced into psychology the notion of finality—the *bête noire* of positivism—, which

[6] Standard Edition, vol. XVI, p. 316.
[7] We take the liberty of referring to our studies: "St. Thomas and the Psychology of Freud"; and "The Moral Act," *supra*, Part I, Chapter I.
[8] Freud, *Three Essays on the Theory of Sexuality,* Standard Edition, vol. VII, pp. 232–233.

commands St. Thomas's whole ethics. (See the very first questions of "IIa Pars" of the *Summa Theologica*.)

We are also indebted to him for having emphasized the dynamism of love and of the search for happiness (another major theme of St. Thomas), and for having shown at the same time that there is a "beyond the pleasure principle," this "beyond" being the reality principle; and this is curiously near Aristotle's position which St. Thomas adopted and brought into play.[9]

We would like to point out one more thing: Freud, besides the fact that he considers procreation as the end of the sexual act, regards as pathological the psychology of Don Juan, and as normal the election of a privileged partner. He takes as cause and effect of all sexual neurosis the dissociation of what he calls the tender, affectionate feelings and the sensual feelings:

When cases of severe psychical impotence are subjected to exhaustive study by means of psychoanalysis, the following psycho-sexual processes are found to be operative. Here again—as very probably in all neurotic disorders—the root of the trouble lies in an arrest occurring during the course of development of the libido to that ultimate form which may be called normal. To ensure a fully normal attitude in love, two currents of feeling have to unite—we may describe them as the tender, affectionate feelings and the sensual feelings—and this confluence of the two currents has in these cases not been achieved.[10]

Freud goes on to assert: "Of these two currents affection is the older. It springs from the very earliest years of childhood."

Another Freudian position which is very interesting for us is the following: as the nervous system is based on the subtle interplay of antagonistic and hierarchical functions which restrains the lower ones in order to integrate them (see the already old work of Hughlings Jackson[11]), likewise Freud recognizes the normal curbing role of the primitive libido. He writes:

The injurious results of the deprivation of sexual enjoyment at the beginning manifest themselves in lack of full satisfaction when sexual desire is later given free rein in marriage. But, on the other hand, unrestrained sexual liberty from the beginning leads to no better result.

9 See *supra*, p. 89.
10 Freud, *Collected Papers*, London, Hogarth Press, 1953, vol. IV, p. 204.
11 Hughlings Jackson, "Croonian Lectures." See Part II, Chapter I, n. 33.

It is easy to show that the value the mind sets on erotic needs instantly sinks as soon as satisfaction becomes readily obtainable. Some obstacle is necessary to swell the tide of the libido to its height; and at all periods of history, wherever natural barriers in the way of satisfaction have not sufficed, mankind has erected conventional ones in order to be able to enjoy love. This is true both of individuals and of nations. In times during which no obstacles to sexual satisfaction existed, such as, may be, during the decline of the civilizations of antiquity, love became worthless, life became empty, and strong reaction-formations were necessary before the indispensable emotional value of love could be recovered. In this context it may be stated that the ascetic tendency of Christianity had the effect of raising the psychical value of love in a way that heathen antiquity could never achieve; it developed greatest significance in the lives of the ascetic monks, which were almost entirely occupied with struggles against libidinous temptation.[12]

Finally—to bring to a close the enumeration of the bases for a dialogue between St. Thomas and Freud—, we would like to briefly point out the subtlety, sometimes indeed hazardous and limited, of Freud's analyses around the theme of the sexual "taboo."[13] They contribute a great deal to a better knowledge of modesty, and at the same time they manifest the profound insufficiencies of the Freudian theses. These theses, in fact, do not go beyond the passional level of fear, which, as we have seen, is not that of the virtue of chastity. This is, at least for the moralist, a radical lacuna in the works of contemporary sexologists and psychologists—which does not prevent the moralist from greatly benefiting by these sciences. The latter are in fact only in their infancy and would not refuse our collaboration if we knew how to work at it seriously.

C. St. Thomas's Principles

Thus, contemporary psychological insights can be very useful to the moralist as well as to the pastor, and especially to those who educate young religious to chastity. It is for this reason that it was necessary, in the beginning, to make a rapid inventory of what psychological

[12] Freud, *Collected Papers,* vol. IV, p. 213.
[13] Note that Aristotle, echoed by St. Thomas, knew already the importance of the attractiveness of incest, to which Freud gave such prominence in his "Oedipus complex"; see IIa IIae 154, 9.

sciences can bring us. If there is a Catholic morality which is able to integrate these new insights, it is indeed that of St. Thomas Aquinas. We would therefore like to recall quite rapidly the essential principles of Thomistic morality, in regard to temperance and chastity.[14]

Temperance is a virtue. This means that it is a dynamism, a sort of spiritual "musculature," of our potentialities to love, a dynamism which is acquired by their exercise and puts our freedom into action. Temperance has as its material object the passions of the concupiscible, especially those of touch and taste, because of their great intensity and extension, since they are linked to the instinct for life, that of the individual as well as that of the species.

The formal object of this virtue is to give these passions a reasonable order. This is to be understood as a harmony of the passional dynamism, a harmonization of all our affective powers, the spiritual powers being called by nature to animate the passional. It is an order, that is to say an ordination, a hierarchical finalization, and it is a reasonable order, that is to say, conformable to the reality of things, subjective as well as objective.

This order of nature was disturbed by the consequences of original sin. The realm of the passions in man, which by nature calls for a harmonization by the mind, does not lend itself easily to it and tends on the contrary, not only to obtain its functional independence, but to draw to itself and to put at its service the rational function.

To win the power due to itself, reason therefore must first temper, moderate the passions. But this moderation is not an end in itself: the final aim of temperance is to integrate the dynamism of the passions into that of the mind. Its aim is absolutely not to suppress, to kill the realm of the passions, but to make it live as is befitting to human nature.

Temperance, therefore, is the fruit of an education of the passions, that is to say, of the joys.[15]

From this position of St. Thomas's ethics, so often ignored, and which finds a confirmation in contemporary psychologies, we will extract only this consequence useful for our subject: the good effect of the virtue of temperance is to make us appreciate—as is fitting—

[14] This exposition will sum up what has been developed in the preceding chapter, pp. 115ff.
[15] See *supra,* pp. 107ff.

passional joys. The "*finis operantis*" of temperance, St. Thomas says, is happiness (IIa IIae 141, 6).

It is, of course, a question of a specifically "human" happiness, that is to say conformable to our nature, to the nature of an animal indeed, but of an animal endowed with reasonable intelligence and with the corresponding affectivity. This enables us to posit "human acts," that is to say acts which presuppose the understanding of things, the disinterested love of the "*bonum honestum*" and of persons for themselves, and finally acts which are free, to which I determine myself on my own impulse.

The moral effort comes down finally to broadening this capacity to posit "human acts" beyond the domain proper to intelligence and its affectivity. It is a question of enabling the realm of the passions itself to become the seat of human acts. The virtue of temperance has in fact for its seat the passions of the concupiscible. This means that it "humanizes" them, that it frees them from psycho-physiological determinism: it allows them, in the very heart of this determinism, a certain self-determination, insofar as the passions succeed in participating, from within and though they remain passions, in the affectivity of the intelligence. This is only possible to the extent that they can subordinate their specific end (enjoyment) to the end of the mind (the happiness of the *bonum honestum*).

One will better understand now why and in what way modesty is not a genuine virtue.[16] It is but a passion, not yet put in order by the reason. It is but a fear which, indeed, can restrain the immoral disorders of concupiscence. But it only restrains, dissimulates. It does not harmonize, it does not integrate, it does not make the concupiscible capable of free acts.

This is true also of the passion which St. Thomas calls *honestas* (IIa IIae 145) and which is but a passional love of moral beauty. It is, one might say, the "sense of honor" with respect to sexual life. As with modesty, its reference is external and social, it is not the *bonum honestum* (Ia Iae 4, 2); it is not by itself capable of human acts.

One will also understand why the virtue of continence is but an imperfect virtue. Its seat is not the concupiscible but the voluntary.

16 See *supra*, p. 126.

The continent man wants himself chaste, he has the understanding of the spiritual love of chastity but his passions are not yet "temperate," they still have desires independent from the reasonable order. They do not order themselves from within to the desires of the mind. There ensues an atmosphere of struggles, even of moral falls. To adopt a very well known comparison that can be found in Aristotle, continence exerts on the passions a police repression which forces them to subversion, to clandestinity, and incites them to revolt, whereas the genuine virtue of chastity grows according to a democratic type of regime, a strong regime indeed, but a regime in which the opposition collaborates for the common good, is won over without compulsion to the legitimate power, is, as English people say, "the opposition of Her Majesty."

The virtue of chastity alone is a virtue in the full sense of the word, because it alone, to adopt the words of St. Thomas, "stamps and impresses" in the concupiscible appetite a disposition, a new form, which surpasses it in its animality, but which gives it its accomplishment in its humanity (*De Virt. in Communi 9c fine*). In a word, the virtue of chastity alone realizes the successful harmonization of the passions, under the inspiration of the mind. All sexual education must aim at this "humanization," at this harmonious integration. This is true for marriage, this is true for consecrated chastity. We do not have to recall the teaching of the Church on this point, for this is not my subject. We only wish to affirm that religious chastity has as its effect, as J.-M. Pohier showed in his article, "*La chasteté sacerdotale,*"[17] a general and exclusive mobilization of our whole affectivity, spiritual and passional, at the service of the kingdom of God and of the love of God. Such is its aim and such must be the concern of religious educators. One can see to what extent the Thomistic conception of the virtue of chastity is in line with this perspective.

This general mobilization does not take place only on the plane of the virtue of chastity. Let us avoid an "atomistic" conception of the virtues, we mean the error of considering them as unrelated entities.

[17] In *Supplément de La Vie Spirituelle*, no. 62 (3ème trimestre, 1962).

161

"*Actiones sunt suppositorum.*" It is the subject who is chaste, it is he who acts and posits chaste acts. He does so with his whole being, and, so to speak, with all his virtues together. Two points of St. Thomas's teaching must be noticed here: the potential parts of the virtue of temperance and the connection of the virtues.

The subjective parts of the virtue of chastity are modesty and *honestas* which are, as we have seen, conditions of its exercise and of the stages of its growth but do not constitute its essence.

The potential parts are the secondary or subsidiary virtues of temperance; they participate in one way or another in its essence. Thus the potential parts of temperance are not only continence, of which we just spoke, but also clemency and meekness, moderation, humility, studiousness, moderation in gestures and dress (IIa IIae 155–169). All these virtues participate in the spirit of temperance and educators in religious chastity must be attentive to them. We are especially thinking of humility, and this is well known, but also of meekness, the specific object of which is to moderate anger and cruelty. Psychiatrists know quite well that cruelty (sadism, for example) often invades more or less pathological sexuality. To moderate anger and cruelty is thus not foreign to the education of chastity and St. Thomas gives us the reason for it.

There is another Thomistic principle from which unfortunately educators and even teachers in morality usually do not draw all the consequences. It is that of the connection of the virtues (Ia IIae 65): one grows in virtue only by growing in them all at the same time. For virtues, in fact, like the fingers of the hand, grow all at the same time in spite of the normal diversity of their size (Ia IIae 66, 2).[18]

All the virtues are connected in justice which is a *habitus* of the will with regard to the others. Now it is clear that sexuality, the language of the body, cannot be conceived without an essential relation with the partner (without forgetting the child). Moreover, it is not a question of justice only in the juridical sense of the matrimonial contract: it is a question of all justice, including general justice, as St. Thomas calls it, which "is in respect of something due to another" (*Justitia est ad alterum,* Ia IIae 60, 3). It is also a ques-

<hr/>

[18] See A. Motte, "La chasteté consacrée et ses connexions," in *Supplément de La Vie Spirituelle,* no. 54 (3ème trimestre, 1960), pp. 291–306.

tion of the potential parts of justice, from the virtue of religion to social virtues. "Temperance without justice," St. Thomas says, "would not be a virtue" (Ia IIae 68, 5). The object of temperance is indeed limited to the moderation, the ordering of the passions of the concupiscible, but the latter, especially when sexuality is concerned, are expressed by acts which are a language to others. "To have relations," as it is said, means to have sexual relations; it means in fact having relations, a relation with another person. Concretely, there is no temperance without justice, for temperance enables us to order our affective-sexual passions in their relations with others and thus to be "just." This right relation to others necessitates, in order to be assured, an inner regulation of our passions.

In the same way all the virtues, and especially chastity, are connected in prudence. This is very obvious and has often been shown.[19] Many things would have to be said also of the connection between the virtue of chastity and the virtue of fortitude, the object of which is to moderate the irascible.

But it is above all necessary to stress the connection of the virtues in charity (IIa IIae 23, 7 and 8). This point is vital for the virtue of chastity, and especially when it is a question of consecrated chastity. For the latter has foundation and is possible only in those men and women who can say with St. John: "So we know and believe the love God has for us" (1 Jn. 4, 16). In those, that is, in whom charity is alive enough for this love—which in itself is not of a passional and sensible order—to be capable of mobilizing the dynamism (unemployed in the consecrated person) of the concupiscible and make it participate in the spiritual and supernatural love. The infused virtue of chastity, the effect of the grace of God, gives indeed a new and supernatural end to the life of the passions, but it does not automatically reduce the resistance of the passions to the natural order. There is no consecrated chastity without an animation by charity, and an animation which operates down to the very root of being in the world of the passions. And let us not forget that charity, while remaining a love for God, is also a love for our brothers and a love for ourselves. Charity thus makes us capable of a love of the others—even a passional love, as is the case of mercy—which animates and purifies our chastity.

[19] See *supra*, p. 139.

2. THE PRINCIPLES OF EDUCATION

A. *The Stages towards Religious Chastity*

The authentic virtue of chastity can be neither easily nor rapidly acquired. We would even think that in the sons of Adam and Eve it is never totally acquired. What man could assert that all his passions, radically and always, entirely and without unconscious ambiguities, spontaneously participate in spiritual love?

Consequently, we must not be surprised if novices and young religious are still far from the virtue of chastity understood in the perfection of its essence. The task of educators is to take them where they stand and to help them pass from modesty and *honestas* to the imperfect virtue of continence, orienting them towards the perfect virtue of chastity.

How is this to be done? It is first a question of listening to them, of allowing them to speak of these questions, of freeing them from their embarrassment, of shedding light.

It seems desirable to us that the educator, while avoiding, of course, inopportune curiosity or inquisitorial questioning, be able to know where each of his novices stands on this point; and this not only in regard to moral faults and "temptations," but also to the whole of attitudes, remembrances, thoughts, imaginations, even dreams. In short, it is desirable that he be able to judge of the moral and psychological quality of his novice.

By moral and psychological quality, we mean the degree of specifically human maturity. This comes down to knowing if the subject, in the order of sexuality as for all the rest, is capable of positing "human acts," to speak like St. Thomas. This capability is the fruit of long evolution, which is never completed. St. Thomas goes as far as to think that rare are those who reach this level of human development (see, for example, Ia 115, 4).

One can find some good criteria of maturity by basing oneself on the specific elements of the human act.[20]

It is an intelligent and reasonable act—an act of the practical reason. Consequently, let us ask ourselves, on this point, if the sub-

[20] See *supra,* pp. 33–34.

ject is really in possession of the facts as they are, and is well adapted to the complex whole of his personal situation and that of the others, in short, if he is reasonable and prudent. Besides, the specific character of intelligence is to extend its gaze to the universal. Is the subject capable of this, especially regarding these questions of sexuality and affectivity?

The human act is an act of the will, an act of spiritual love, a love of the *bonum honestum,* and not of the useful and the pleasant taken as an end. What exactly is the attitude of our novice with regard to the vow of chastity? Does he really love religious chastity and with which love? With the passional love of *honestas,* or with the spiritual love of the virtue of chastity? Or again is he above all as it were compelled to chastity by the passional fear of modesty? To judge of this, let us beware of words. For it happens that subjects are mistaken about themselves and deceive us in giving back ideas they read or heard and behind which their true motivations are hidden. How difficult it often is to listen to an interlocutor, beyond the words, and to allow him to express himself totally and truly.

A human act is a free act, that is to say an act of which I am the principle, to which I determine myself of myself, of which I am master, author and responsible; this presupposes a choice. What is the value of the choice of religious chastity? Has the subject acquired sufficient maturity and autonomy on this point (as well as on the others, for everything is linked together)?

The human act which the virtue of chastity enables us to posit is an act, not of willing itself, but of passion. It is a participation of the passional in the voluntary, through which the passion itself, of itself, is capable of positing a human act in the specific sense of the word. If the subject is not yet this far along, then he is still under the regime of the imperfect virtue of continence. We will help him to progress, not only by making him discover the reasons for loving chastity spiritually (it is in this way that the imperfect virtue of continence grows and is purified), but also by helping him to "convert" his very passions, to "humanize" them, to "supernaturalize" them.

On this point there are no recipes.

The more frequent obstacles come, it seems to us, from modesty, a modesty which does not want, which cannot give way to the progression towards the genuine virtue of chastity. This passional fear of social and public sanction, this passional guilt is but a childish prefiguration of genuine sexual morality. It is natural at the first stage of moral effort, but it must give way to a more "human" behavior: the virtue of continence and even more the virtue of chastity. In the latter, modesty is as it were absorbed. The genuinely chaste man is no longer afraid of sexual realities (except, of course, if this danger is objectively real); he loves, in his mind and in his passions, the moral beauty of chastity.

But it often happens that modesty does not give way to chaste love and moral progress is thereby stopped or distorted.

This is especially noticeable in people who masturbate and who are otherwise full of good will. They are incontinent and not intemperate. The proof is that, the fault once committed, they are crushed with shame (modesty); the fear of falling again makes them anxious, and thus an obsessional process is established, hardens and hurls them headlong into a new fall—which only increases their anxiety. Thus exacerbated, fear acts somewhat like the dizziness which seizes one in the mountains: the abyss draws one down, it is fear, the panic of falling which would make one fall. One would do exactly what one does not want to do, of which one is afraid—and with what fear!—and exactly because one is afraid of it. In such moments considerations of reason and common sense are totally ineffectual. It is thus necessary to try to dedramatize, in him who masturbates, this fear, this panic; to teach him to distinguish authentic moral culpability—contrition and penance (which are for their part reforming and liberating)—from this passional culpability which on the contrary enslaves him. It is necessary to have him discover the authentic reasons which condemn masturbation: it is a narcissistic eroticism. As we have said, the sexual act is a language of the body; now when one speaks, one speaks to somebody. He who masturbates is a man who speaks to himself. In doing so, he hurts himself; for he stops in himself the felicitous evolution of the affectivity of the child towards the oblativity of the adult. And as everything is linked, he supports at the same time one of the major obstacles to his openness towards the others, to his charity towards the others as well as towards God.

Another misdeed of modesty prolonged in the adult is the excess of guilt in a subject who experiences some trouble or temptation. We are speaking of one who torments himself to measure exactly the degree of his consent, accuses himself with exaggeration and anxiety, confesses and confesses again. It is a more subtle obsession, but it too blocks the progress towards the virtue of chastity. It is then necessary to help the subject to accept the fact that such primary movements exist in him; he must be assured that he is not a monster, but that on the contrary, it is normal, especially for somebody who does not have any affective or sexual relationship, to experience from time to time this very natural need, as it is normal, for instance, after a somewhat long fast to feel the discomfort and the gnawing pain of hunger: if, then, a good smell of stew happens to tickle the nostrils, the feeling of hunger gets stronger; one begins to imagine the next meal and salivation starts. Has one for this broken the fast? No, as long as one has not eaten. Is it a moral fault to feel this hunger? All depends on the use one makes of it; but it is not in itself bad. One can make good use of it, in repeating, for example, one's intention of offering to God. To have excessive fear of the primary movements of sexuality, is on the contrary, to excite it in the worst way and to make more difficult its "humanization" as well as its "supernaturalization." Humility is here in close connection with chastity.

But it happens that in some subjects, this fear is so strong that it forbids practically any liberation of it. This is then in the pathological domain—which would in itself deserve a large development.

We would like only to suggest here a preventive solution.

B. The Testing of the Psychological Aptitudes for Religious Chastity

When a religious experiences, in the observance of his vow of chastity, serious difficulties, which can go as far as the most serious faults, even scandal and the abandonment of the religious life, the cause for it is very often of pathological order.

The harmonious integration of the passional life with the mind has proved impossible, in spite of the good will of the subject, his efforts and those of his educators. For one has here come up against a pathological obstacle which the grace of God, miracles excepted, does not have as its effect to cure, just as it does not cure tuberculosis or a broken leg. We are afraid that, as soon as it is a question of psychological illness, some Catholics fall into the same errors as the followers of Christian Science or the Jehovah's Witnesses.

In these painful cases, psychotherapy is generally to be recommended. But this is often difficult and hazardous. It would have been preferable, it seems, for this psychotherapy to have been undertaken and carried out successfully before admission to the novitiate. And all the more so since the neurosis could have gravely contaminated or distorted the attractiveness of the religious life. It happens then that the—neurotic—attractiveness of the religious life would disappear with the neurosis, and in that event the situation of the subject engaged definitively is dramatic.

As a preventive measure, the introduction before admission of a test of the psychological aptitudes for the religious vocation is to be desired, whenever it is possible. It is in fact the desire of the Church which has been expressed particularly in Article 33 of the *Statuta Generalia* annexed to the apostolic constitution *Sedes Sapientiae.*[21]

On this point of chastity among others, the advantage of such a test is to reveal in time all kinds of latent pathologies in the affective-sexual potentialities. It makes possible the recommendation for appropriate care when it seems necessary and thereby the improvement of the quality of the soil where the grace of religious vocation takes root and develops.

Moreover, when there is no serious pathology, but only slight but tenacious psychological difficulties, or alarming affective immaturities, the psychological test may bring about a favorable awareness of their problems in the subjects, and may allow the examiners to give appropriate advice to the candidate, even to his future father master. The novitiate will thus bear all its fruits. This is a good consequence which we could observe in the institutions where this test is offered to all the candidates.

[21] A. Plé, "An Experiment in Discernment of Vocation," in *Journal of Religion and Mental Health,* January 1962, pp. 165–179.

C. *The Education of the Educators*

Schools for leadership do not exist in the Church and in the religious life, especially with regard to novice masters and masters of scholastics. They are usually chosen among the best religious, but we are not sure that one is always sufficiently concerned with their pedagogical qualities.

These qualities presuppose first, particularly in regard to religious chastity, that the educators themselves be at ease with these problems, that they have acquired good health and good psychological as well as supernatural maturity. It is necessary that they be able to stand the dialogue with their novices on these "delicate questions," that they stand it without being consciously or unconsciously disturbed by their personal problems, and that they be able to educate the chastity of their subjects, adapting themselves to each of them.

This presupposes a certain psychological knowledge. We are thinking especially of psychopedagogy, psychopathology, group psychology; we will add that it would be desirable that this psychological knowledge be integrated with their moral, ascetic, and mystical theology.

Finally, theoretical teaching has its dangers. I think that they can be avoided by using means of education which complete and correct mere information. These means are well known: case work, training groups, individual supervision, etc. They have already proved themselves here and there, and one would wish them to be introduced more generally.[22]

But let us come back to the subjects themselves and insist on the role of charity in an authentic education for religious chastity.

D. *Charity, the Animator of Religious Chastity*

"It is not good that the man should be alone" (Gen. 2, 18). This assertion of God, which gives us the reason for the human couple, also sheds light on consecrated celibacy.

[22] See especially A. Godin, *La relation humaine dans le dialogue pastoral,* Bruges, Desclée de Brouwer, 1963. L. Beirnaert, "Aide et dialogue," in *Etudes* (septembre, 1962), and "Formation au dialogue d'aide," in *Etudes* (juin, 1962). See also R.-M. McKeon, "Les relations humaines dans la vie religieuse," in *Supplément de La Vie Spirituelle,* no. 62 (septembre, 1962), and Harold C. Bradley, "Une session de psychologie pastorale," in *ibid.*

It is not good for the religious to be lonely. A certain type of solitude threatens first his chastity. The latter is genuine, possible and fruitful only if the religious is not alone in life. He must then be with God, and in a sufficiently strong and active way so that, even in his sensitivity, he be not alone. This is truly supernatural, for the love of God is not of a passional order. We believe in the love of God; this means that we do not have the evidence for it; neither rational, nor sensible evidence. It is given to us, indeed, to have a certain experience of the love of God, but this experience is even more tenuous and intangible than the "small still voice" which Elijah heard on Mount Horeb (1 Kgs. 19, 12).

The consequence of celibacy is therefore a very profound affective frustration. Celibacy places us, so to speak, in an atmosphere where respirable oxygen is lacking. There is no solution but in a love of God, not experienced at the "fundus of the soul," but extending to our whole being, including the world of the passions. Besides, it is certainly in this way that charity grows in us (IIa IIae 24, 5).

If this is not assured, religious chastity turns against the one who has vowed it; either he dries up and becomes the "old bachelor" religious; or else he suffocates, and becomes the religious more or less unfaithful to his vow. By this fact, there is no genuine religious chastity without a prayerful life, without an ever growing and purifying faith in the love of God, without a certain "connaturalness" with the divine realities, without the experience of a "relation" with God. The religious must be able to make his own, *mutatis mutandis,* this word of our Lord: "And he who sent me is with me; he has not left me alone, for I always do what is pleasing to him" (Jn. 8, 29).

Not less important are the life in common, the relations between brothers, for here also charity is exercised and grows. The life in common is like the sacrament of the love of God. Charity animates and sanctifies in it the relations of human friendship, and thus removes the religious from a solitude, which I would call secondary with regard to God, but the fortunate or unfortunate working of which is most important as far as religious chastity is concerned.

A last point in conclusion. The apostolic ministry brings into action charity, the love of neighbor. In one way or another, charity is exercised in it, not only in the general intention already present in the motivations of the vocation and which can be repeated every day, but in the very moment, in the very act in which this ministry is exercised. To love one's neighbor, not only in our morning resolutions, but when he is there, and to love him with the entire capital of charity which has been given to me, this is the ideal. Everyone gains by it: my neighbor, for my charity in exercise is for him like a sacrament of God who is Charity, and I myself, who am very close to God, in divine relation with God and at the same time with my neighbor.

Such a fraternal and apostolic charity presupposes profound purifications of our affective, especially our passional, powers. Psychotherapists know quite well—and this is why a psychoanalyst, for example, should first have been analyzed—that it is not easy to be as it were affectively "neutral," and at the same time kind towards every patient. Neutral does not mean absent, but rather free from one's own affectivity. It is not easy to place oneself "at the proper distance" with regard to the other; neither too close, for this would result in identifying oneself with him and as it were absorbing him; nor too far, for this would mean no longer listening to him, helping him, loving him.

We would have, we believe, for a better exercise of our charity, some good lessons to receive from psychotherapists, and especially from the specialists in counseling and non-directive therapy.[23]

Be that as it may, it is certain that the virtue of chastity, because it ensures the integration of our passions in charity, is called to be exercised and to grow in our ministry, and that, moreover, charity finds in it a most efficacious purifying agent.

Indeed, there is no consecrated chastity without charity, and in return, charity profits by our chastity. The religious state is defined by the tending towards evangelical perfection, that is to say, essentially towards charity. It is the *raison d'être* of religious chastity, it is its truth and its fecundity. The whole problem is that it be an authentic virtue of chastity such as it presents itself in the light of St. Thomas.

[23] See, for example, the work, in French, of Carl Rogers and G. Marian Kinget: *Psychotherapie et relations humaines,* vol. I: *Exposé général,* Louvain, Publications Universitaires, and Paris, Béatrice Nauvelaerts, 1962.

Conclusion

Charity and the Unity
of the Affective Life

MORALITY, as we kept repeating throughout this essay, is a matter of love, pleasure, in short, of affectivity.

The moral success of a man is summed up, finally, in the quality of his love. It is a question of loving the good well. Of loving the good, rightly appreciated as it is concretized in the multiple goods which are the objects of our affectivity, spiritual as well as sensible; and of loving the good well, that is to say in a graded integration of all our potentialities of love and in a movement regulated by the "reality principle."

The basic truth of "natural" moral life is both confirmed and exalted beyond itself by the "royal law"; we have recalled, at the beginning of this work, its precept in which everything is summed up and accomplished: "You shall love."

Christian morals have their source and end in charity: "You shall love the Lord your God with all your heart, and with all your soul, and with all your mind. This is the great and first commandment. And a second is like it, You shall love your neighbour as yourself. On these two commandments depend all the law and the prophets" (Mt. 22, 37–40). These are the only commandments whose observance—the Church has taught this to us from its first response to our petition for baptism—makes us enter into Life: "Do this, and you will live" (Lk. 10, 28). Charity is, according to the expression of St. James, the "royal law" (Jas. 2, 8).[1]

[1] All the New Testament texts on charity are collected in the volume *L'amour du prochain*, Paris, Editions du Cerf, 1954, pp. 62–113.

The formulation of the Lord's precept is by itself rich in lessons. We learn by it particularly whom we must love: God, our neighbor, ourselves. The extent and the unity of such a love deserve attention and wonder.

Theologians are used to accounting for it by saying, following St. Thomas, that charity has as its formal object the goodness of God. Charity makes me love the infinite goodness of God, which is eminently and totally found in God, but also, in a sort of reflexion, in my neighbor. Then this formal object is materialized in two concrete objects: God first, but also my neighbor (beginning with myself).[2]

I love my neighbor because he loves God (or in order that he love God), because God lives in him[3] and molds his ways on his own (or in order that God may do so). By loving him in that way, I love my neighbor in the most secret part of his person, which cannot find its truth but with regard to God, that is to say insofar as he is created by God and is capable of beatitude, which consists in enjoying God.[4] By charity I love my neighbor in his reference to God; it is thus God whom I love in him; charity is essentially a love of God.[5]

All this is true, but when one reads St. Thomas closely, one finds that he completes this teaching or rather makes this abstract truth concrete. Thus, after having specified that charity is to be situated in the noblest kind of our human affections, friendship, and that the foundation of the latter is a sharing,[6] St. Thomas teaches that the foundation of charity is a *"communicatio"* of beatitude. He speaks in turn of a *"quaedam consociatio in beatitudine"*—"a sort of society of beatitude" (IIa IIae 25, 12), of a *"communicatio beneficiorum pertinentium ad vitam aeternam"*—"communication of the treasures which belong to eternal life" (IIa IIae 25, 10), of a *"communicatio spiritualis, per quam ad beatitudinem pervenitur"*—"spiritual sharing by which one attains beatitude" (IIa IIae 25, 3), and of a *"communicatio donorum gratiae"*—"communication of the gifts of grace" (IIa IIae 26, 3). By charity God is loved as the cause of

[2] See IIa IIae 25, 1. [3] *De Caritate,* 4c.
[4] *De Caritate,* 8c.
[5] *De Caritate,* 9, ad 5; see 4, ad 2; 4, ad 7; 8, ad 16.
[6] IIa IIae 23, 1.

beatitude, and the neighbor *"sicut beatitudinem simul nobiscum ab eo participans"*—"because together with him we participate, through God, in beatitude" (IIa IIae 26, 2); etc.[7] This is why, in spite of its many different objects, charity is a unique virtue; for it has but one foundation: the *communicatio* of beatitude.[8] Charity is the love of the common good of this heavenly society in which Christ gives us the right of citizenship (Eph. 2, 19), the love of the heavenly Jerusalem.[9]

By nature, already, we must love God above all, since, being our creator, he is the principle and the end of the Good.[10] How much more then, by charity, we must love God above all things "as he is the object of beatitude, and inasmuch as man has a spiritual fellowship with God" (Ia IIae 109, 3).

Dealing with the object of charity, manuals *ad mentem sancti Thomae* generally forget to mention this spiritual society spoken of by St. Thomas, profoundly faithful here as elsewhere to the sources of our faith. For we know, particularly through St. John, that men are called to enter with the divine persons into a "community" (κοινωνία) (1 Jn. 1, 1–7) and in a "unity" which leaves the faithful overwhelmed: "That they all may be one; even as thou, Father, art in me, and I in thee; that they also may be in us . . . ; that they may be one even as we are one: I in them and thou in me, that they may become perfectly one" (Jn. 17, 21–22).

Concretely, charity is thus the love of this community of beatitude in which the divine persons are united, and, in Christ, charity realizes the unity with them of the human persons who are "called." Charity is the "link" (Col. 3, 14) of this Unity; it makes it (Eph. 4, 16). The Father and the Son are "bound" between them by the Spirit of love;[11] the members of the mystical body of Christ are linked to the divine persons and at the same time to one another by the charity "poured into our hearts through the Holy Spirit" (Rom.

---

[7] IIa IIae 26, 2. See also IIa IIae 25, 3; 25, 6; 25, 10; 1; 2; 3; etc.
[8] IIa IIae 23, 5.   [9] *De Veritate, 2.*
[10] See IIa IIae 26, 3; Ia 60, 5.
[11] The Holy Spirit is the "knot," the "bond," the "kiss" of the Father and the Son. These images are classical in the Fathers of the Church. See Ia 37, 1, ad 3. See H. F. Dondaine, "Notes doctrinales," in *La Trinité,* vol. II, p. 399, of the edition of the *Somme* (édition de la *Revue des Jeunes*).

5, 5), in the charity through which the Church is built (Eph. 4, 16), and especially by the Eucharist whose fruit is charity.[12] By greeting one another with a "holy kiss,"[13] the members of Christ participate in this unity which the Father and the Son seal between them by the "Kiss" of the Holy Spirit.[14]

The object of charity is thus, concretely, that divine beatitude common to the three divine persons and which, in the body of Christ, places us "in fellowship" with them and with all our brothers. Charity is the love of the common good of this fellowship of the blessed, it makes us admire and love this good for itself, it makes us desire its diffusion and its triumph.[15]

The unity of this love parallels its extent. He who has charity loves, all in one, the divine persons and all the human (and angelic) persons who are called to beatitude and constitute the Church, militant, suffering, and triumphant. This immense object of charity constitutes a whole which cannot be dissociated. To be sure, the analysis of the theologian is useful, which studies separately the exercise of charity towards God and that which makes us love our neighbor. The fact remains that, concretely, charity towards God cannot be dissociated from charity towards our brothers. To speak of charity is even normally to designate it in the fullness of its object, it is to speak of our love in God for our brothers.[16] Such is the habitual usage of the New Testament and the Fathers. Not being able to quote here all these texts, and especially those of St. Paul, we will only refer here to the following text of St. Augustine:

How can each one know that he has received the Holy Spirit? Let him ask his heart: "If he loves his brother, the Holy Spirit abides in him." Let him see himself, let him test himself under the regard of God: let him see if there is in him the love of peace and unity, the love of the Church spread over all the earth.[17]

Charity is the love of the Church and of all its members in a unity in the process of becoming. Charity does not have an abstract

---

[12] See *La Maison Dieu,* no. 24: "La Messe, engagement de charité."
[13] 1 Cor. 16, 20; 2 Cor. 13, 12; 1 Pet. 5, 14.
[14] St. Bernard, *Sermon 8 on the Canticle,* no. 2.
[15] *De Caritate,* 2.   [16] IIa IIae 27, 2.
[17] St. Augustine, *Homilies on the Gospel according to St. John,* VI, 10.

object (divinity, divine Goodness); it is not even enough to say that it makes us love the living God, living but inaccessible in his absolute transcendence: it makes us love God in and by what is very concretely human, in the Church and each of our brothers.

"If any one says, 'I love God,' and hates his brother, he is a liar; for he who does not love his brother whom he has seen, cannot love God, whom he has not seen" (1 Jn. 4, 20). One's neighbor is in a way a sacrament, a "mystery"; in letting himself be seen and loved, he gives us God as object of love. "You have seen your neighbor, you have seen your God."[18] "He who has seen me has seen the Father" (Jn. 14, 9): it is the same mystery.[19] Thus, by charity—insofar as its plenary object and exercise include the neighbor—"a new light of the glory of the Father shines in the eyes of our mind, in such a way that, knowing God visibly, we are thereby ravished in the love of invisible things" (Preface of Christmas).

If our charity is in this way essentially "mysteric," it is because it is as divine as it is human in a unity which does not exist only on the symbolic plane, but also in its ontological reality.

Charity is divine, for "God is love" (1 Jn. 4, 9), and if some charity can exist between men, it is only from God that it can proceed: "Love is of God" (1 Jn. 4, 7). "God's love has been poured into our hearts through the Holy Spirit which has been given to us" (Rom. 5, 5), "love that is in Christ Jesus" (1 Tim. 1, 14).

At the same time, charity is human not only through the "mysteric" value of the neighbor, but also with regard to its object: it makes us love men, all men and each of them in particular, from within, where God calls him to absolute happiness. Finally, charity does not make us love only the souls, but also the bodies and all the material goods that it makes us desire "to God's honor and man's use."[20]

Charity is also human with regard to its subject and this for three reasons: the Christian loves himself with charity, charity is a love, and a love which tends to invade the whole subject.

[18] Clement of Alexandria, *Stromates*, I, 19, 94, and II, 15, 71 (*PG*, 8, 812 and 1009); Tertullian *De Orat.*, 26 (*PL*, 1, 1193). See also the *Apophtegmes des Pères* (Apollon., 3; *PG*, 65, 136).

[19] See A. Plé, "Le prochain, mystère de Dieu," in *La Vie Spirituelle* (octobre, 1945).

[20] IIa IIae 25, 3; see IIa IIae 32, 2–4.

1. The Christian must love himself with charity; he is for himself the closest neighbor. Without this love of himself, it is impossible to have charity, for it is impossible to love one's neighbor without having oneself entered this "society of beatitude" on which charity is founded. It is first necessary to love this beatitude and have for oneself the love which is strong and pure enough to make us enter it, in order to be able to love all those who are called to share it with us.[21]

Indeed, charity presupposes renunciations. It makes us renounce moral evil, and even authentic goods, such as the life of the body,[22] but these are demands stemming from a spiritual love of ourselves and not from any unconscious masochism to which some psychoanalysts would like to reduce Christian morality. Catholic morality is a very human morality, for this main reason, that it demands from man that he love himself, with the same love with which God loves him, and that this love of oneself lead up to and give support to the love of our brothers. "You shall love your neighbor as yourself" (Mt. 22, 39). "So whatever you wish that men would do to you, do so to them" (Mt. 7, 12).

2. It is not only because charity has as its object the subject himself that Catholic morality is profoundly human: it is so also because of the central place it gives to love. It thereby finds support in the dynamism of human life, in the universal aspiration of men who are made to love. It is, St. Thomas says, in the joy of love that man finds the perfection of his being.[23]

We need to love and to be loved. To know that we are loved, were it only by one person, is for us a vital necessity. The little child needs it in order to develop normally, and the adult finds in it his accomplishment. Now faith gives us the certitude that we are loved by God: "We love, because he first loved us" (1 Jn. 4, 19); "See what love the Father has given us, that we should be called children of God; and so we are" (1 Jn. 3, 1); "In this the love of

[21] IIa IIae 26, 4. The natural love of God, also, is founded on the love of ourselves; see Ia 60, 5.

[22] "By this we know love, that he laid down his life for us; and we ought to lay down our lives for the brethren" (1 Jn. 3, 16).

[23] In Gal., 5, 6.

God was made manifest among us, that God sent his only Son into the world. . . . not that we loved God but that he loved us" (1 Jn. 4, 9–10).

But charity, like all love, consists even more in loving than in being loved.[24] This is what charity enables us to do, in a way which surpasses our best aspirations. There is indeed, in all our affections, even the virtuous ones, a certain self-seeking,[25] but we sense quite well that we are called to surpass this interested love and to love the others for themselves: the perfection of love incites us to a total oblativity and gratuitousness. It is then that we love the Good for itself and persons for themselves[26] and that, having forgotten ourselves, we reach moral perfection and at the same time full psychological health. *"He who loses his life finds it."* Charity is such a love: come from God, it perfects man in all his nobility, and at the same time it meets, cures and raises in him the very impetus of life.

Thus charity makes us capable of a total oblativity towards God and our brothers with whom, at the same time, it makes us one.[27] For love, the love of friendship which is charity, is "ecstatic": he who loves, St. Thomas says, is as it were drawn out of himself, being as it were transferred into him whom he loves, to whom he wishes good and gives it by his care, as for himself.[28] Love is "ecstatic," love is also "unitive": it is union in its cause, in its essence and in its effect.[29]

[24] IIa IIae 27, 1.

[25] This love which St. Thomas calls love of concupiscence is not necessarily sinful: it is first a law of our nature (see IIa IIae 19, 6). This is true even with regard to our love for God: insofar as it is from him alone that we can receive happiness, the love we have for him is not disinterested; it is nonetheless this love on which is founded the theological virtue of hope.

[26] The Thomistic analysis distinguishes two objects in love: the good loved and the person for whom one wants this good; this rejoins the distinction of the honest good on the one hand, and of the useful and delectable good on the other. Friendship is a love of the honest good, it ends up with a person, loved for himself and in this case loved without any reference to anything else; he is on the contrary the reference for the goods which one wants for him. See Ia IIae 26, 4.

[27] Charity which we have for ourselves participates also in this objectivity: through charity we love ourselves in a very real way, but in the profound truth of our vocation—which is not one of the least benefits of charity.

[28] Ia 20, 2, ad 1   [29] Ia IIae 28, 1 ad 2.

3. Charity makes us love God, ourselves and our brothers, with all the richness of our being: "You shall love . . . with all your heart, and with all your soul, and with all your might," Deuteronomy said already.[30] It is the entire man who loves with charity.

St. Thomas's moral theology is here particularly enlightening. It makes of charity a virtue, that is to say, a *habitus*.[31]

There are *habitus* of the intelligence, of the will, of the effectivity. For St. Thomas, charity is a *habitus* of the will. By this word, we must understand our spiritual power to love—something like the passion of the mind—, and not the imperious, dry, and drying tension, the tyrannical constraint of oneself to which custom, for several centuries, has reduced the meaning of this word.[32]

For St. Thomas, the will is a love, an appetite for the goods perceived by the intelligence;[33] it thus has all the dynamism of love and at the same time all the qualities of the mind. When a man surpasses the level of affectivity and is being born to the life of the spirit, what he loves then, his reason for living, the end which he gives to himself is the object of his will—which directs itself too, though secondarily, towards all the means which he uses and towards all the intermediary stages which mark out his road towards the final object of his love. Charity then takes root in us, in our spiritual

[30] Deut. 6, 5. The reader is referred to the very interesting study of Antoine Guillaumont on "Les sens des noms du coeur dans l'Antiquite," in *Le coeur* ("Etudes Carmelitaines," 1950), which establishes that in the Semitic language (and therefore in that of the New Testament, too) the heart is not the seat of the affectivity, but of the "whole of the moral and spiritual being" (p. 66). Moreover, the second term of this trilogy must be understood as the "psyche." Therefore, in order to be faithful to the primitive text, we moderns should translate: "with all your soul, with all your psyche, with all your strength."

[31] See *supra*, pp. 117ff.

[32] The history of the language would here be very enlightening. It would reveal all that language lost of its conception and of its perception of the human reality during the Renaissance. This is what the short note of M. D. Chenu on the affective categories in the language of scholasticism suggested already (*Le Coeur, op. cit.,* pp. 123–128). Chenu points out in particular a passage of St. Thomas (in his commentary on the precept of charity: "You shall love . . . with all your heart"), for whom the heart means here the will (IIa IIae 44, 5). For St. Francis de Sales, the will is the intellectual or reasonable love. See *The Love of God,* Westminster, Newman, 1963, Book 5 and *passim.*

[33] See Ia 1, 82; Ia IIae 6; etc.

capacity to love.[34] In doing so, charity cures and raises our will, for it is a supernatural *habitus:* it is "infused" in us by God,[35] and thus enables our will to love God as "the object of beatitude and inasmuch as man has a spiritual fellowship with God."[36]

Thus this love, divine by its source and its object, takes root really in our internal dynamism. This divine mode of loving is all the more human. This is so true that it is in both these directions that the growth of charity takes place.

Like all virtue, charity demands growth.

Natural virtues may grow in two ways: according to a new extension of their object (that is, the apprentice geometrician who understands a new theorem), or according to the greater and greater depth at which these *habitus* take place in the subject and perfect him (that is, science which invades the whole life of the scientist).[37]

Charity cannot know an extension of its object: it is total or it does not exist; it makes us love all persons, divine and created, united in the same beatitude. To except the most miserable of these persons, is to cease to have charity: "He who observes in his heart a trace of enmity towards somebody, because of some offense, is completely foreign to the love of God. Love of God and hate for a man are in every way incompatible."[38]

Since this is so, charity can grow in us only according to the greater depth at which it takes root. "The likeness of the Holy Spirit," St. Thomas says, "is more perfectly participated by the soul."[39]

---

[34] Ia IIae 24, 1; *De Virt, in com.,* a, 5.

[35] The result of this is that, contrarily to natural *habitus,* charity does not grow by being exercised: it is a gratuitous gift of God, in the initial gift as well as in its growth. The Christian does not grow in charity by the sole play of his own strength. His role is limited to asking for this growth through prayer. In exercising his charity, however, he disposes himself to receive a greater gift, and he deserves to receive it (IIa IIae 24, 6).

[36] Ia IIae 109, 3, ad 1.   [37] See Ia IIae 52, 1.

[38] St. Maximus Confessor, *Capita de caritate,* I, 15.

[39] IIa IIae 24, 5, ad 3. We can only notice here the importance of charity in the play of the gifts of the Holy Spirit and especially of the gift of wisdom. St. Thomas accounts for the latter by showing that it gives a knowledge of God almost experiential by connaturalness: when charity is great, it serves as a medium of knowledge of him who is Charity (IIa IIae 45, 2). Commenting this text, the spiritual authors speak only of charity

To grow in charity is to love more and more as God loves and at the same time to do so by an act ever more intimate, personal, free, and strong. The charity of God is destined to invade our whole being, not only in our will, but also in all our powers.

This is what St. Thomas shows by stating that charity is the "form" of our virtues.[40] This means that charity does not merely make us love God through the proper acts of our spiritual love ("elicited" acts of our will), it demands to inspire all our other affections ("imperated" acts of our will), that is to say, all our virtues.[41]

As perfectly as they are exercised, each in its direction, our virtues demand to participate in this higher love of which charity makes the will capable. For example, justice keeps its specific object (the love of equity), but it demands, in order to be an absolutely perfect justice as well as to perfect the just man according to the call of God, to be as it were "super-motivated" by charity. It is not to a man but to a brother that the Christian does justice; it is not only through love of equity, it is through love of beatitude.

It is thus that, rooted in the will, charity exerts on our other faculties a sort of radiance, an attraction, a seduction, but also a domination.[42] By grouping them around it, by putting them at the

---

towards God. It would be good to know that charity towards our brothers has the same effect. Thus it is St. Paul's prayer that "love [for our brothers] may abound more and more, with knowledge and all discernment" (Phil. 1, 9). See Col. 2, 2: "that their hearts may be encouraged as they are knit together in love, to have all the riches of assured understanding and the knowledge of God's mystery, of Christ, in whom are hid all the treasures of wisdom and knowledge."

[40] Cf. Ia IIae 23, 7 and 8; *De Caritate*, a. 3. See Deman, "La charité fraternelle comme forme des vertus," in *La Vie Spirituelle* (mars, 1946). St. Thomas says also that charity is root, motor, and mother of the virtues (Ia IIae 62, 4; *De Caritate*, a. 3) and that it "produces" their acts (*De Caritate*, 2, ad 14).

[41] The object of virtue is always some aspect of the good which is, by definition, object of the love of an upright mind. See Ia IIae 55, 1, ad 4.

[42] This *"imperium"* of charity must not be conceived in a voluntaristic way. It consists, for the will, in acting on the other virtues by "calling" them to tend towards the end of charity (*De Caritate*, 5, ad 3), in "ordering" them to an end which is superior (*De Caritate*, 3, ad 18). A simple judgment of the mind is sufficient for this, for the will inclines naturally to what the judgment of reason shows to it as a good (*De Virt., in com.*, 5,

service of its love, it promotes them, it liberates them and raises them above themselves. Through charity and through it alone, our virtues receive a sanctifying value: without charity the just man is only an honest man, with charity, he is "divinized" in his being and in his behavior; his justice is molded on that of God, which, because it is *the* Justice, is not really distinct from his Being which is Love.

It would be useful to show in detail all that this animation of charity brings to the exercise of our virtues: to religion, to justice and the social virtues, to fortitude, temperance, and prudence itself. Theologians carefully distinguish and classify all these virtues but will they never show us their concrete exercises under the *imperium* of charity? St. Paul shows them the way when, in his "hymn to charity," he attributes to it, with so much insight, the qualities of all the virtues. It is thus written that charity is willing to help, it does not act indecently, does not seek its own profit, etc. (social virtues), it does not boast and does not swell with pride (humility), it is patient and bears everything (virtue of fortitude), it believes everything (virtue of faith), and hopes everything, etc.[43]

What is true of our virtues is also true of our passions. Our passional affections, our whole affectivity also asks to be assumed by charity. It is especially the case of mercy,[44] which by itself is a passion but which, animated by charity, is raised to the nobleness of virtue. Unbelievers are "without tenderness," St. Paul says (Rom. 1, 31); on the contrary, the Christians are *made tender* by charity (Rom. 12, 10). If they are far from one another, they "are desirous" of one another (2 Cor. 9, 14) in the "affection of Christ Jesus" (Phil. 1, 8).

St. Thomas asserts that sensible affection sprung from charity orients itself towards its perfection[45] and that all legitimate natural

---

ad 1). The love of the will radiates then naturally on the powers of love of the senses. If it has to impose upon them this supermotivation, it does so through the strength of its love.

[43] 1 Cor. 13, 4–7. See Eph. 4, 25 (truthfulness); 1 Thess. 5, 13 (obedience); Phil. 1, 9 (conduct); 1 Cor. 6, 15 (charity); Gal. 5, 6 (faith); etc. Charity is "religious," for it is obedience to God: *"animas vestras castificantes in obedientia caritatis"* (1 Pet. 1, 22).

[44] IIa IIae 30, 3.

[45] *De Caritate,* 11, ad 8.

affections must be animated by charity.[46] This is so true that, when he establishes the hierarchy of the charity which we must have towards our neighbor, one of the two principles he uses is the neighbor's natural closeness to the subject: the links of blood, the belonging to one and the same social body are the foundations not only for a primacy in natural love, but for the hierarchic order of our charity.[47] The Christian must love (with charity) his parents, his wife, his children, his fellow citizens more intensively, not only because they are more immediately called to participate with him in divine beatitude, but also because of the natural love he has for them, which charity must assume. The more we love them with natural love, St. Thomas says, the more we have to love them with charity.

It is thus our whole being, from the most spiritual faculties to the most psychical, which demands to be animated by charity. It is precisely this which constitutes the growth of our charity according to its imperated acts. As for the elicited acts (that is to say, the very acts of charity), their growth is realized in the sense of a greater intensity and of a greater identification with our most profound self, and at the same time a greater conformity to the divine mode of loving.

For all these reasons, charity is our great safeguard against sin. He who has charity, insofar as he acts through the strength of this love, cannot sin.[48] Were a man able to love with charity without stopping he would no longer be able to sin. This is the case of the blessed in heaven. It is by essence, St. Thomas says, that charity is able to make us resist temptation,[49] for "the sovereign remedy against sin is that man come back to his heart and convert it to the love of God."[50]

"Sin is lawlessness" (1 Jn. 3, 4), but sin, which destroys man, uses the law to give us death;[51] charity alone destroys sin and gives us life: "We know that we have passed out of death into life, because we love the brethren" (1 Jn. 3, 14). It is charity which unites us to God, and which resorbs in us the love of sin.[52] This is why the seriousness of sin is measured with regard to charity: if the attrac-

---

[46] De Caritate, 7; 8; 9 and 9, ad 12.   [47] IIa IIae 26, 7.
[48] De Caritate, 12.   [49] De Caritate, 10, ad 4, and 5, ad 7.
[50] De Caritate, 12, ad 9.   [51] See Rom. 7, 13.
[52] De Caritate, 6, ad 8.

tiveness of sin, without directly opposing the movement of charity, nonetheless keeps it from being exercised, there is venial sin; if, on the contrary, the love which makes us act is opposed to charity, there is mortal sin.[53] To sin is to love wrongly; sin is a "sickness of the soul."[54]

This rapid and no doubt incomplete inventory of the treasures of charity (as well as of the morality which it founds) seems to me to be able to satisfy the most demanding wishes of contemporary moralists and psychologists: internal and progressive dynamism of love and virtue which are exercised in joy;[55] harmonization, on every psychological level, of our multiple forces, which are coördinated with one another by a higher love and united in it; ever more personal, autonomous, total, easy, adapted, and constant commitment; total oblativity and intimate union with regard to the persons of an immense fellowship, fecundation of the law, and social constraint by love.

Christian morality is at once superhuman, supernatural, divine (for charity comes from God and molds us after him); it is finally Christian and ecclesial, that is to say, that we receive it from Christ of whom we are members, and that it is the internal law of structure and growth of the society of the blessed. In short, Christian morality, in its object as well as in its exercise, unites the divine and the human and gives them to us in their unity. It would be none of this if it were not essentially a love.

---

[53] See Ia IIae 88.   [54] Ia IIae 88, 1.

[55] It is a question of that joy which is the specific effect of charity and which is as it were its "fruit" (Ia IIae 70; *In Gal.*, 5, 6). It is also a question of the joy which the exercise of all *habitus* gives (see pp. 83ff.).

Index of Authors Cited

185

Subject Index

Absolute, 74

Acedia, 91

Act, elicited, imperated, 43, 181, 183; free, 25, 60, 118–119, 165

Act(s), human, 28–43, 57, 66, 72, 74–75, 86, 95, 160, 165; and the action of man, 28, 41; coincides with moral act, 28–29, 32, 35; essence of, 28–33, 35–36; first, 51–52; and Freud, 54–56, 66–71, 98; genesis of, 50–54; integration of the person, 41–43, 49, 55–57, 59–60, 75, 118, 120, 127, 137; specific qualities of, 33–41, 84, 165; *See* Act, moral; Inferior analogues of the human act; Sin and first human act; and the summons of God, 34; and the world of passion, 71, 126–127, 159; *See* Passion, participle of virtue

Act, moral, 24–75, 119; according to St. Thomas, 24–26, 28–33, 98; *See* Act, human

Act, sexual, 140, 142, 145–146, 148, 155, 166

Adolescence, 51, 65

Adult, 55, 105, 128, 134

Affectivity, spiritual, 29, 79, 81, 96; and sensible, 29, 54

Age of reason, 51, 64

Aggressiveness, 55, 70, 100, 156

Analogy, 52–53, 72

Animal psychology, 153

Appetite, 33–34, 82, 91–93, 100; intellectual or spiritual, 41, 58, 72, 84–86; natural, 81–82, 85–86, 100; sensible, 38, 40, 42–43, 45, 58, 81–82, 85–86

Assumption, 64

Autonomy, 15, 33, 65

Beatitude, 37–39, 49–50, 65, 94–96, 108, 116, 121; communication of, 173–174, 177, 180

Being, concept of, 53; and goodness are "convertible," 79

Charity, 16–19, 29–30, 77, 119, 163, 172–184; "form of all virtues," 54, 60, 120–121, 146, 181–183; growth of, 181–184; *See* Chastity and charity; Consecrated chastity and charity

Chastity, ability to love, 147–148; according to St. Thomas, 161–162; and charity, 142, 145–147, 163, 166; Christian, 143–149; education to, 150–171; and faith, 144–146; and hope, 145–146; and humility, 138, 162, 167; and justice, 139–

187